First World War
and Army of Occupation
War Diary
France, Belgium and Germany

39 DIVISION
116 Infantry Brigade
Royal Sussex Regiment
13th Battalion
5 March 1916 - 14 August 1918

WO95/2582/3

The Naval & Military Press Ltd
www.nmarchive.com
Published in association with The National Archives

Published by

The Naval & Military Press Ltd

Unit 10 Ridgewood Industrial Park,

Uckfield, East Sussex,

TN22 5QE England

Tel: +44 (0) 1825 749494

www.naval-military-press.com

www.nmarchive.com

This diary has been reprinted in facsimile from the original. Any imperfections are inevitably reproduced and the quality may fall short of modern type and cartographic standards.

© **Crown Copyright**
Images reproduced by permission of The National Archives, London, England, 2015.

Contents

Document type	Place/Title	Date From	Date To
Heading	13th Battalion Royal Sussex Regiment.		
Heading	116th Brigade 39th Division France.13th Battalion Royal Sussex Regt.1916 Mar-1918 Aug, Absorbed Bs 1/4 R Sussex.		
Heading	13. B 711 Bde 39 Div 9 Dec-Dec 1917		
Heading	116th Brigade. 39th Division. Battalion Disembarked Havre 6.3.16. 13th Battalion The Royal Sussex Regiment March 1916		
Heading	13 R Sussex Vol 1		
War Diary	Milford. Eng.	05/03/1916	05/03/1916
War Diary	Havre.	06/03/1916	07/03/1916
War Diary	Steenbecque	08/03/1916	08/03/1916
War Diary	Morebecque	08/03/1916	11/03/1916
War Diary	Neufberquin	11/03/1916	11/03/1916
War Diary	Rue Du Quesnoy	12/03/1916	18/03/1916
War Diary	Sailly Sur La Lys	19/03/1916	19/03/1916
War Diary	Fleurbaix	20/03/1916	22/03/1916
War Diary	Estaires	23/03/1916	25/03/1916
War Diary	Robermetz	25/03/1916	25/03/1916
War Diary	Verte Ruc	31/03/1916	31/03/1916
Heading	116th Brigade. 39th Division. 13th Battalion The Royal Sussex Regiment April 1916		
War Diary	Verte Ru	01/04/1916	13/04/1916
War Diary	Locon	14/04/1916	14/04/1916
War Diary	Givenchy	15/04/1916	30/04/1916
Heading	116th Brigade. 39th Division. 13th Battalion The Royal Sussex Regiment May 1916		
War Diary	Hinges	01/05/1916	09/05/1916
War Diary	Festubert	09/05/1916	25/05/1916
War Diary	Hinges	26/05/1916	28/05/1916
War Diary	Cuinchy	28/05/1916	31/05/1916
Heading	116th Brigade. 39th Division. 13th Battalion The Royal Sussex Regiment June 1916		
War Diary	Cuinchy	01/06/1916	10/06/1916
War Diary	La Pannerie	11/06/1916	16/06/1916
War Diary	Ferme Du Bois	17/06/1916	23/06/1916
War Diary	Vielle Chapelle	23/06/1916	27/06/1916
War Diary	Ferme Du Bois.	28/06/1916	30/06/1916
Operation(al) Order(s)	Operation Order No 23	28/06/1916	28/06/1916
Miscellaneous	Appendix A. Communications.		
Miscellaneous	Appendix B		
Miscellaneous	Operation Order No. 25		
Heading	116th Brigade. 39th Division. 13th Battalion The Royal Sussex Regiment July 1916		
Heading	War Diary of 13th Div R. Suss. R. From July 1st 1916 To 31st July 1916 Vol 5		
War Diary	Vielle Chapelle	01/07/1916	05/07/1916
War Diary	Bethune	06/07/1916	07/07/1916
War Diary	Annequin South	08/07/1916	11/07/1916
War Diary	Cuinchy	12/07/1916	14/07/1916

War Diary	Le Touret	15/07/1916	20/07/1916
War Diary	Ferme Du Bois	21/07/1916	24/07/1916
War Diary	Rue L'Epinette	25/07/1916	27/07/1916
War Diary	Festubert	28/07/1916	31/07/1916
Operation(al) Order(s)	Operation Order No 35	30/07/1916	30/07/1916
Heading	116th Brigade. 39th Division. 13th Battalion The Royal Sussex Regiment August 1916		
Heading	War Diary of B Bn R Suss. R From 1st August 1916 To 31 August 1916 Vol 6		
War Diary	Festubert	01/08/1916	01/08/1916
War Diary	Essars	02/08/1916	06/08/1916
War Diary	Gorre	07/08/1916	11/08/1916
War Diary	Lozinghem	12/08/1916	13/08/1916
War Diary	Magnicourt-En-Comte	14/08/1916	22/08/1916
War Diary	Moncheaux	23/08/1916	23/08/1916
War Diary	Ivergny	24/08/1916	24/08/1916
War Diary	Bois Du Warnimont	25/08/1916	27/08/1916
War Diary	Wood (P.17) Near Mailly-Mailly	28/08/1916	31/08/1916
Heading	116th Brigade. 39th Division. 13th Battalion The Royal Sussex Regiment September 1916		
Miscellaneous	Headquarters 116th Infantry Brigade.	01/10/1916	01/10/1916
War Diary	Wood (P.17) Near Mailly Maillet	01/09/1916	02/09/1916
War Diary	Hamel	03/09/1916	03/09/1916
War Diary	Prowse Fort	04/09/1916	04/09/1916
War Diary	Wood P 17	05/09/1916	06/09/1916
War Diary	Bertrancourt	07/09/1916	09/09/1916
War Diary	Beaumont Hamel Sector	10/09/1916	14/09/1916
War Diary	Mailly-Maillet	15/09/1916	18/09/1916
War Diary	Redan Ridge	19/09/1916	30/09/1916
Heading	116th Brigade. 39th Division. 13th Battalion The Royal Sussex Regiment October 1916		
Heading	War Diary of 13th Bn Royal Sussex. For The Month Of Oct 1916 Vol 8		
War Diary	Redan Ridge	01/10/1916	03/10/1916
War Diary	Y. Ravine	04/10/1916	09/10/1916
War Diary	Englebelmer Wood.	10/10/1916	12/10/1916
War Diary	Redan Section	13/10/1916	15/10/1916
War Diary	Redoubt Right Section	16/10/1916	21/10/1916
War Diary	Redoubt Section	21/10/1916	21/10/1916
War Diary	Stuff Trench	21/10/1916	22/10/1916
War Diary	Martinsart Wood	23/10/1916	24/10/1916
War Diary	Schwaben Redoubt	25/10/1916	27/10/1916
War Diary	North Bluffs.	28/10/1916	30/10/1916
War Diary	Left River Section.	30/10/1916	31/10/1916
Miscellaneous	Secret O.T Bys 13th Royal Sussex Regt.	19/10/1916	19/10/1916
Heading	116th Brigade. 39th Division. 13th Battalion The Royal Sussex Regiment November 1916		
Heading	War Diary of 13th Bn Royal Sussex Regt Nov 1st 1916 To Nov 30th 1916 Vol IX		
War Diary	Pioneer Rd	01/11/1916	05/11/1916
War Diary	River Centre Section.	05/11/1916	06/11/1916
War Diary	Martinsaart Wood	07/11/1916	13/11/1916
War Diary	Thiepval	13/11/1916	15/11/1916
War Diary	Authieulle	16/11/1916	18/11/1916
War Diary	L Camp Poperinghe	19/11/1916	30/11/1916

Heading	116th Brigade. 39th Division. 13th Battalion The Royal Sussex Regiment December 1916		
Heading	War Diary of 16th Bn. Royal Sussex Regt For The Month Of December 1916 Vol 10		
War Diary	L Camp Poperinghe	01/12/1916	12/12/1916
War Diary	Turco Farm	12/12/1916	14/12/1916
War Diary	Turco Fm Section.	15/12/1916	18/12/1916
War Diary	Canal Bank	19/12/1916	20/12/1916
War Diary	Hill Top Farm Section.	21/12/1916	24/12/1916
War Diary	G Camp Poperinghe	24/12/1916	29/12/1916
War Diary	Boesinghe Reserve.	30/12/1916	30/12/1916
Heading	13th Bn Royal Sussex Regt War Diary For The Month Of January 1917 Vol XI		
War Diary	M Camp.	01/01/1917	11/01/1917
War Diary	Boesinghe.	11/01/1917	20/01/1917
War Diary	Railway Wood	20/01/1917	31/01/1917
Heading	War Diary For The Month Of February 1917 13th Bn R. Sussex Regt Vol XII		
War Diary	Railway Wood	01/02/1917	03/02/1917
War Diary	O Camp.	04/02/1917	24/02/1917
War Diary	St. Lawrence Camp	24/02/1917	28/02/1917
Heading	War Diary of 13th Bn R. Sussex Regt For March 1917. Vol 13		
War Diary	Observatory Ridge Sector. The Bund	01/03/1917	03/03/1917
War Diary	St. Lawrence Camp	04/03/1917	09/03/1917
War Diary	Observatory Ridge Sector.	10/03/1917	13/03/1917
War Diary	Kruisstraat.	14/03/1917	17/03/1917
War Diary	Observatory Ridge Sector.	17/03/1917	21/03/1917
War Diary	St Lawrence Camp	22/03/1917	28/03/1917
War Diary	Observatory Ridge	28/03/1917	31/03/1917
Heading	War Diary of 13th Bn R. Sussex R. For April 1917 Vol 14		
War Diary	Observatory Ridge	01/04/1917	04/04/1917
War Diary	Ypres	05/04/1917	06/04/1917
War Diary	St. Lawrence Camp	07/04/1917	11/04/1917
War Diary	Hodge Sector.	12/04/1917	18/04/1917
War Diary	Hill Top.	18/04/1917	30/04/1917
War Diary	Bouvelingham Training Area	01/05/1917	15/05/1917
War Diary	St. Martin Au Laert	15/05/1917	15/05/1917
War Diary	Buysscheure	16/05/1917	16/05/1917
War Diary	Wormhoudt	17/05/1917	31/05/1917
War Diary	Canal Bank	01/06/1917	04/06/1917
War Diary	La Brique	05/06/1917	10/06/1917
War Diary	Canal Bank.	11/06/1917	16/06/1917
War Diary	Lancashire Fm.	17/06/1917	21/06/1917
War Diary	O Camp.	22/06/1917	22/06/1917
War Diary	Houlle.	23/06/1917	16/07/1917
War Diary	Z Camp	17/07/1917	21/07/1917
War Diary	A 30 Group Camp	22/07/1917	29/07/1917
War Diary	Canal Bank.	30/07/1917	30/07/1917
War Diary	Assembly Trenches	31/07/1917	31/07/1917
War Diary	St. Julien And Black Line	01/08/1917	02/08/1917
War Diary	Canal Bank.	03/08/1917	03/08/1917
War Diary	School Camp.	04/08/1917	07/08/1917
War Diary	Pichboom	08/08/1917	11/08/1917
War Diary	Ridgewood	12/08/1917	13/08/1917

War Diary	Bois Confluent.	14/08/1917	17/08/1917
War Diary	Hollebeke Sector.	18/08/1917	21/08/1917
War Diary	Bois Confluent	22/08/1917	23/08/1917
War Diary	Ridge Wood	24/08/1917	27/08/1917
War Diary	Klein Zillebeke	28/08/1917	08/09/1917
War Diary	Shrewsbury Forest.	09/09/1917	13/09/1917
War Diary	Ridgewood	14/09/1917	15/09/1917
War Diary	Shrewsbury Forest.	16/09/1917	19/09/1917
War Diary	N.9.6	20/09/1917	25/09/1917
War Diary	Tower Hamlets	26/09/1917	27/09/1917
War Diary	Frontier Camp.	28/09/1917	14/10/1917
War Diary	Tower Hamlets Sector.	15/10/1917	19/10/1917
War Diary	Beggars.	20/10/1917	20/10/1917
War Diary	Rest Camp.	21/10/1917	23/10/1917
War Diary	Broke Camp.	24/10/1917	28/10/1917
War Diary	Murrumbidgee Camp	29/10/1917	02/11/1917
War Diary	Tower Hamlets (Left Front And. Section)	03/11/1917	06/11/1917
War Diary	Canada Street.	07/11/1917	07/11/1917
War Diary	Chippawa Camp.	08/11/1917	08/11/1917
War Diary	Murrumbidgee Camp.	09/11/1917	16/11/1917
War Diary	Scottish Wood Camp.	17/11/1917	19/11/1917
War Diary	Bedford House Camp.	20/11/1917	25/11/1917
War Diary	Winnizeele	26/11/1917	29/11/1917
War Diary	Ypres	30/11/1917	30/11/1917
War Diary	Wieltje	01/12/1917	08/12/1917
War Diary	Steenvoorde	09/12/1917	10/12/1917
War Diary	Coulomby	11/12/1917	31/12/1917
War Diary	Siege Camp.	01/01/1918	06/01/1918
War Diary	Hilltop Farm	07/01/1918	14/01/1918
War Diary	Westroosebeek Sector.	15/01/1918	18/01/1918
War Diary	Hilltop Farm.	19/01/1918	19/01/1918
War Diary	Corps Line.	20/01/1918	21/01/1918
War Diary	School Camp.	22/01/1918	26/01/1918
War Diary	Sailly Laurette.	27/01/1918	30/01/1918
War Diary	Haut Allaines	31/01/1918	01/02/1918
War Diary	Church Camp Heudicourt.	02/02/1918	04/02/1918
War Diary	Right Front Sub-Sector	05/02/1918	18/02/1918
War Diary	Divisional Reserve	19/02/1918	22/02/1918
War Diary	Right Front Sub-Sector	23/02/1918	28/02/1918
Heading	116th Inf. Bde. 39th Div. War Diary 13th Battn. The Royal Sussex Regiment March 1918		
War Diary	Right Front Sub Section.	01/03/1918	20/03/1918
War Diary	2nd Battalion Of Somme	21/03/1918	31/03/1918
Heading	39th Division. Composite Brigade 116th Brigade. Formed Part Of No. 2 Composite Battalion 10.4.18. 1/13th Battalion Royal Sussex Regiment April 1918		
War Diary	Guignencourt.	01/04/1918	12/04/1918
War Diary	Chateau Segard.	13/04/1918	16/04/1918
War Diary	Wytschaete	16/04/1918	20/04/1918
War Diary	Walker Camp	21/04/1918	21/04/1918
War Diary	Dominion Camp	22/04/1918	25/04/1918
War Diary	Spoil Bank	25/04/1918	26/04/1918
War Diary	A.20 Camp.	27/04/1918	29/04/1918
War Diary	Dominion Camp	30/04/1918	01/05/1918
War Diary	Green lines Dickebusch Area	02/05/1918	05/05/1918
War Diary	Nielles Les Ardres	06/05/1918	24/05/1918

War Diary	Bonningues.	25/05/1918	07/06/1918
War Diary	Licques	08/06/1918	17/06/1918
War Diary	Grasse Payelle	18/06/1918	22/06/1918
War Diary	Listergaux.	23/06/1918	01/07/1918
War Diary	Grasse Payelle	02/07/1918	25/07/1918
War Diary	Licques	26/07/1918	14/08/1918

13TH BATTALION ROYAL SUSSEX REGIMENT

116TH BRIGADE
39TH DIVISION

FRANCE

13TH BATTALION

ROYAL SUSSEX REGT.

~~JAN - DEC 1917~~

1916 MAR — 1918 H&G

ABSORBED BY 1/4 R SUSSEX

Dec 1917

116th Brigade.
39th Division.

Battalion disembarked HAVRE 6.3.16.

13th BATTALION

THE ROYAL SUSSEX REGIMENT

MARCH 1 9 1 6

AA/39

13 R Sussex

Vol 1

Army Form C. 2118.

WAR DIARY
or
INTELLIGENCE SUMMARY.
(Erase heading not required.)

Place	Date	Hour	Summary of Events and Information	Remarks and references to Appendices
	1916. March.			
Milford.Eng.	5	—	Left WITLEY CAMP by 3 trains. Embarked from SOUTHAMPTON. 860 on S.S. "VIPER". 1120 on S.S. "AUSTRALIND". Good crossing.	RBMc
HAVRE.	6	—	Disembarked and marched to No. 5 Rest Camp. Snow.	RBMc
"	7	7AM.	Entrained.	RBMc
STEENBECQUE	8	3.30AM	Detrained and marched to Rest Camp, MOREBECQUE	RBMc
MOREBECQUE	8-11		In Rest Camp. (Hqrs D.14.b.2.6.) FRANCE 36A.	RBMc
NEUFBERQUIN	11		Marched as Brigade from MOREBECQUE to NEUF BERQUIN. In Billets for night. (Hq.G.24.d.98)	RBMc
RUEDUQUESNOY.	12		Marched from NEUF BERQUIN to RUE DU QUESNOY, via ESTAIRES and SAILLY Sur La LYS. (Hq.G.24.d.9.8) "A" & "C" Cos. in Trenches attached to 2ⁿᵈ Rifle Brigade & 2ⁿᵈ Royal Berkshires respectively. Each Platoon attached to a Company and distributed along its front.	RBMc
"	13		"A" & "C" in 25 Platoons. "B" & "D" Supplied Working Parties. 1 man Wounded on Working Party.	RBMc
"	14		"B" & "D" relieved "A" & "C". Attached to 2ⁿᵈ Rifle Brigade, & 2ⁿᵈ Lincolns. Distributed as on 12ᵗʰ.	RBMc
"	15		"B" & "D" in by Platoons. "A" & "C" supplied Working Parties.	RBMc
"	16		"A" & "C" relieved "B" & "D" and took over Company Fronts from 2ⁿᵈ R.B's & 2ⁿᵈ Lincs respectively.	RBMc
"	17		"A" & "C" in 25 Companies. "B" & "D" as Working Parties. 2 Men Wounded on Working Parties.	RBMc

Army Form C. 2118.

WAR DIARY
or
INTELLIGENCE SUMMARY.
(Erase heading not required.)

Instructions regarding War Diaries and Intelligence Summaries are contained in F. S. Regs., Part II. and the Staff Manual respectively. Title pages will be prepared in manuscript.

Place	Date	Hour	Summary of Events and Information	Remarks and references to Appendices
	March 1916.			
RUE DU QUESNOY	18		"B" & "D" relieved "A" & "C" and took over Company frontages. 1 Man wounded.	
SAILLY SUR LA LYS	19		Marched to SAILLY sur La LYS. (Hq. G.16.d.3.0) In Billets for night. "B" & "D" Left Trenches and marched to Billets.	
FLEURBAIX	20		Marched to FLEURBAIX. In reserve to 11th Bn. R.Suss. R. "A" Coy in CROIX MARECHAL POST. "C" Coy in CAIN POST	
	21			
	22			
ESTAIRES	23		Relieved by 16th Bn. Royal Scots. Marched to Billets in vicinity of ESTAIRES. (HQ. L.17.d.4.8)	
ROBERMETZ	25		Moved to Billets on NEUF BERQUIN- MERVILLE Road. (HQ. K.24.d.3.6) FRANCE 36A.	
	24			
VERTE RUE	31		Moved to Billets. (Hqrs. E.28.d.4.3.)	

T./134. Wt. W708-776. 500000. 4/15. Sir J. C. & S.

116th Brigade.
39th Division.

13th BATTALION

THE ROYAL SUSSEX REGIMENT

APRIL 1 9 1 6

WAR DIARY or INTELLIGENCE SUMMARY.

Army Form C. 2118.

(Erase heading not required.)

D.2

Place	Date	Hour	Summary of Events and Information	Remarks and references to Appendices
VERTE RUE	1916 April 1-13		In Billets. Hors. E.28.d.4.3 (Map 36A). Company and Specialist training carried on & daily Baths. was inspected by XI Corps Commander. Lt. Gen. Sir R. HAKING, K.C.B. accompanied by G.O.C. 39 Div. Maj Gen N.W. BARNARDISTON H.M.O. on April 3rd. The Bn. was highly complimented on its turn out & smartness. During the whole of this period exceptionally fine weather prevailed.	
LOCON	14		Moved from VERTE RUE to LOCON via MERVILLE. Billeted about LOCON for the night. Brig Gen. J.E. WATSON C.B. relinquished command of the 116 Bgde after being in command for just over a year. Brig Gen. H.L. HOFKYN D.S.O. assumed command.	
GIVENCHY	15		Moved from Billets about LOCON and took over right sub Sector of GIVENCHY Area, relieving 13th Bn. Royal Welch Fusiliers. The Bn. moved in via GORRE and the LA BASSÉE Canal, moving by Sections at 50 yards distance from GORRE onwards. Reliefs commenced at 9 AM and were complete by 11.20 AM. The line was taken over by Companies as follows:- "A" Coy (Captain S. HUGHES) high Breastwork in the part of trench known as the DUCKSBILL. "B" Coy (Captain M.J.N. MAKGILL) centre Coy. "C" Coy (Captain C.M. HUMBLE CROFTS) right Coy. "C" Coys right extended to North Bank of the Canal. "D" Coy in PONT FIXE Keep in Support. Trenches were found to be in a very poor condition. Wire in front of parapet practically non-existent. Wherever	

Army Form C. 2118.

WAR DIARY
or
INTELLIGENCE SUMMARY.
(Erase heading not required.)

Instructions regarding War Diaries and Intelligence Summaries are contained in F.S. Regs., Part II. and the Staff Manual respectively. Title pages will be prepared in manuscript.

Place	Date	Hour	Summary of Events and Information	Remarks and references to Appendices
GIVENCHY	15		Immediately started to remedy damaged defects, chiefly building dugouts and closing gap in the parapet between "B" & "C" Coys. The day was quiet with the exception of exchange of Rifle Grenades and 1 Man wounded. Patrols went out all night to examine Enemy's wire. Good results were obtained. Lieut. C.A.F. WHITLEY sent in an excellent report about now. Inspected by G.O.C. 39" Divn. Machine Guns in right sector were active at night — The 14th Bn HAMPSHIRE Regt occupied the left subsector & 12th Bn. ROYAL SUSSEX REGT in support in villages etc.	
	16		Fine day. Enemy shelled GUNNERS SIDING, and VILLAGE LINE in morning. No material damage was done — At about 12.30 p.m. he made an attempt hit on our parapet in "B" Coys trenches, killing and wounding 10 men. A great number of Rifle Grenades was fired on both sides. Enemy Machine Guns were active all night. Patrols were sent out at night & accounted for two Huns. A large amount of work was done on front part of the line. Total casualties 5 killed and 16 wounded.	
	17		Enemy very quiet all day with exception of firing a few Rifle Grenades at night, but Machine Guns were very active. We fired a large number of rifle grenades	

T.134. Wt. W708-776. 500000. 4/15. Sir J.C. & S.

WAR DIARY or INTELLIGENCE SUMMARY.

Army Form C. 2118.

Instructions regarding War Diaries and Intelligence Summaries are contained in F. S. Regs., Part II. and the Staff Manual respectively. Title pages will be prepared in manuscript.

(Erase heading not required.)

Place	Date	Hour	Summary of Events and Information	Remarks and references to Appendices
GIVENCHY	APRIL 1916 17 cont		in reply to rifle & M. Gun enemy Sn rifle & M.G. were continually active at night sweeping the roads behind the enemy's lines. Our patrols were active at night in spite of the bright moonlight. Their men kept busy working parts but a wounded and fell upon the road. Our wounded Lce Corpl Dick & Pte Tebarne were under fire killing Lce.Cpl.P.McROBERTS (who had stayed with the wounded). Lt.Grubbs went out for him and recovered him. One of us Lgunlich men Pte DARVIN and HAYTER who were carrying out the rescue were killed. A large amount of work was done on the parapet.	
	18		A quiet day with the exception of the usual exchange of rifle & M.G. fire. Patrols active at night. A considerable amount of work done on wire and parapet.	
	19		Battalion relieved by 11th Bn R.SUSS.R. Bn moved back to GORRE in 38th Reserve April at GORRE CHATEAU	
	20.21 22		In Billets in GORRE. Whole time devoted to cleaning up equipment and kit and general personal kit.	

WAR DIARY or INTELLIGENCE SUMMARY.

Army Form C. 2118.

(Erase heading not required.)

Instructions regarding War Diaries and Intelligence Summaries are contained in F. S. Regs., Part II. and the Staff Manual respectively. Title pages will be prepared in manuscript.

Place	Date	Hour	Summary of Events and Information	Remarks and references to Appendices
GIVENCHY	April 1916 23		Relieved 1/4 Bn. R. SUSS. R. in right sub-sector. Reliefs commenced at 7 A.M. The Companies left in the same positions with the exception that "D" took over the DUCK'S BILL sector and "A" went into Reserve at PONT FIXE. The usual exchange of Rifle Grenades took place. The enemy dropped a few 12/15 Shells close to Bn. Hdqrs. but had no damage. Our damages not highly personal. Work on Trenches continued. Bombing of Snipers and great many Grenades.	
	24		Enemy shelled Bn. O.P. at GUNNER STREET and GIVENCHY the usual Grenades and M.G. activity took place at Break plant Bn. overnight kept steady. had shown the gap between B. & C. Carefully shelled. Patrol went out again at night. 1/4 ALTAR/ALTGR. reported to be a Bomb Store & enemy wire. Total casualties. Officer & 3 men wounded	
	25		Quiet day with the exception of a few rifle Grenades fired followed into "D" Coy's trenches and killed one man and wounded through M.P. General front line enemy works carried out. Others also at night. Total Casual Ray Ut. 1 killed and many 5 wounded	
	26		Enemy quiet all day with the exception of a few Rifle Grenades.	

Army Form C. 2118.

WAR DIARY
or
INTELLIGENCE SUMMARY.
(Erase heading not required.)

Place	Date	Hour	Summary of Events and Information	Remarks and references to Appendices
GIVENCHY	26		Fairly cold again. There has been N.G. on both sides but latterly a light patrol was active. Working parties went out but no shelling was done. Aeroplanes and sniping very active.	TEM
GIVENCHY	27		Relieved by 11th Bn. R. SUSS. R. The Battalion took over F. VILLAGE LINE as Battalion in support. Companies distributed as follows — A & C in Pillars in Village. B Coy in LEPLANTIN KEEP and WINDY CORNER. D Coy in GIVENCHY KEEP, HERTS REDOUBT, MOATFARM, and HILDERS REDOUBT. Day spent refitting and cleaning up. Keeps occupied by D were frequently shelled during the day.	TEM
	28		All Coys. as in working parties day and night. GIVENCHY KEEP again shelled. No casualties or any material damage done. At about 8.40 P.M. a Gas Alarm was sounded on our right. The whole Battalion went to Alarm post for two hours luckily the gas did not reach our sector.	
	29		All Coys on working parties. Slight shelling of Keeps at helpers. The wind again being favourable for the enemy every precaution was	TEM

T.134. Wt. W708—776. 500000. 4/15. Sir J. C. & S.

Army Form C. 2118.

WAR DIARY
or
INTELLIGENCE SUMMARY.
(Erase heading not required.)

Instructions regarding War Diaries and Intelligence Summaries are contained in F. S. Regs., Part II. and the Staff Manual respectively. Title pages will be prepared in manuscript.

Place	Date	Hour	Summary of Events and Information	Remarks and references to Appendices
	April 1916			
ANNEQUIN	29		Relief of the Battalion	
	30		Battalion relieved by 1/4th Black Watch 118th Bgde. Battalion marched back to billets about LA PANNERIE. Headquarters at PONT LHINGES (N.4.C.3.7.) BETHUNE COMBINED SHEET.	

Y.W. Chalmers Lt. Col.
Commdg. 13/13 R. Rifles.

116th Brigade.
39th Division.

13th BATTALION

THE ROYAL SUSSEX REGIMENT

M A Y   1 9 1 6

Army Form C. 2118.

WAR DIARY
or
INTELLIGENCE SUMMARY.

(Erase heading not required.)

13th Bn ROYAL SUSSEX REGt VOL 3

Place	Date	Hour	Summary of Events and Information	Remarks and references to Appendices
HINGES	1916 MAY 1-9		In Billets about LA PANNERIE, in Divisional Rest. All men were refitted where necessary. Daily training was carried out of all Specialists and Coys.	
FESTUBERT	9		Relieved the 17th Bn Kings Royal Rifle Corps in the FESTUBERT Left Sub-Sector. "A" Coy took over the right and "D" Coy the left. "C" Coy and "B" Coy were in Support in Old British Line.	
	10		Day very quiet. In the evening wiring parties were out. An enemy patrol came close to Island 30A and threw two bombs which did no damage and then retired.	
	11		A few "Whizz-Bangs" were sent into RICHMOND TCE but did little damage. In the evening enemy M.G's were very active, and considerably hampered our wiring parties. An enemy patrol again approached Island 30A and threw bombs to which our bombers replied driving the enemy off. L/Sgt HARRIOTT, Bn H'n Sniping Sergt killed by M.G. fire. This splendid N.C.O. will be greatly missed. Work carried out on wire and reclamation of SHETLAND ROAD Communication Trench.	

Army Form C. 2118.

WAR DIARY
or
INTELLIGENCE SUMMARY.
(Erase heading not required.)

Instructions regarding War Diaries and Intelligence Summaries are contained in F. S. Regs., Part II. and the Staff Manual respectively. Title pages will be prepared in manuscript.

Place	Date	Hour	Summary of Events and Information	Remarks and references to Appendices
FESTUBERT	MAY 1916 12		Enemy was unusually quiet along our whole front line during the day and night. Wiring parties on both sides were very busy. 2 Lt E. SPARKS took out a patrol to try and find 2 men A."D"Coy who were missing from the previous night. Unfortunately no trace of the missing men was found. General Trench maintenance was carried out on our work in SHETLAND ROAD TRENCH.	PRR
	13		Except for a few Whizz Bangs directed against Right Centre Coy. which did no damage, enemy very quiet all day. Relieved by 11th Bn R.Suss.R. returning to Billets at LE TOURET.	PRR PRR
	14-15-16		In Billets at LE TOURET. Working parties daily.	
	17		Bn relieved the 11th Bn R. Suss. R. in the Left Sector. "B" and "C" Coys. taking the right and left respectively in the front line. "A" Coy in Support in the Old British line. Enemy very quiet during our relief. No Casualties. Our Winnie Squeak put out a large quantity of wire.	PRR
	18		Enemy very active day and night with Snipers and M.G's.	

T.134. Wt. W708—776. 500000. 4/15. Sir J. C. & S.

WAR DIARY or INTELLIGENCE SUMMARY

Army Form C. 2118.

Place	Date	Hour	Summary of Events and Information	Remarks and references to Appendices
FESTUBERT	May 1916 18		Own M.G's replied effectively, silencing the enemy on several occasions. Own Wiring Parties were busy erecting new wire and strengthening the old. Work on Parapet and new B.H'rs Bomb Store carried out.	
"	19		Usual Sniping activity by day, and M.G's at night, otherwise nothing to report. Wiring Squads put out 91 coils of wire. Reclamation work carried out in SHETLAND ROAD Trench, in addition to general maintenance.	
"	20		Enemy very quiet, day and night. 2 Whizz Bangs dropped within ten yards of Bn Hqrs. No damage. Our Snipers were active and claim 2 victims. Wiring Parties again did very good work putting out 112 coils of wire. 2nd Lt G.E.ELLIOTT, Battn Signalling Officer killed this Officer had done splendid work in training the Battalion Signallers taking great pains to bring them up to their present high state of efficiency.	
"	21		Except for a few "Whizz Bangs" in the afternoon enemy very quiet all day. It's Snipers and M.G's were also inactive. Bn relieved by 11th Bn	

T.134. Wt. W708—776. 500000. 4/15. Sir J. C. & S.

Army Form C. 2118.

WAR DIARY
or
INTELLIGENCE SUMMARY.
(Erase heading not required.)

Instructions regarding War Diaries and Intelligence Summaries are contained in F. S. Regs., Part II. and the Staff Manual respectively. Title pages will be prepared in manuscript.

Place	Date	Hour	Summary of Events and Information	Remarks and references to Appendices
FESTUBERT	May 1916 21		R.Sus.R., Relief successfully carried out without casualties. Bn moved into Kepi and Rifle in FESTUBERT VILLAGE LINE.	
"	22.23.24		Bn in FESTUBERT VILLAGE LINE in Support. Repairing to Kepi and Billets carried out.	
"	25		Bn relieved by 7/S⁺ Bn Black Watch. Bat'n moved to Billets about LA PANNERIE. Bn H.Q. at POINT CHINGES. Lt.Col. F.G.W. DRAFFEN proceeded on leave. Capt S.Hughes [By Command] Army	
HINGES	26.27		In Billets. First day devoted to cleaning up and rest. Second day dressing parades on the Divisional Training Area.	
"	28		At 3.15 P.M. orders were received that the Bn had to relieve the 2ⁿᵈ ARGYLE & SUTHERLAND HIGHLANDERS, 98ᵗʰ INF B.G.DE, 33ʳᵈ DIV'N in the CUINCHY LEFT Sector. Bn moved off at 6.30 PM marching via LOCON and GORRE. Relief complete by 12.15AM. Companies were allotted as follows:- In the front line "B" right, "C" centre, "A" left, "D" Coy in Support. Bat'n Hqrs at "KINGSCLERE".	
CUINCHY	29		Bat wn 10 and 11 A.M. the enemy sent over several H.E.'s and Whizz Bangs, blowing in a portion of COLDSTREAM LANE Communication Trench. At night	

WAR DIARY
or
INTELLIGENCE SUMMARY.
(Erase heading not required.)

Army Form C. 2118.

Place	Date	Hour	Summary of Events and Information	Remarks and references to Appendices
GUINCHY	29		An enemy raiding party succeeded in entering a small portion of "C" Coy front. The raid was preceded by an heavy bombardment on our front and support line trenches. Parapet was damaged in several places. 6 Casualties. The raiding party succeeded in capturing a N.C.O and several rifles. A demonstration was also made by parties of the enemy in front of "B" and "A" Coys. They were met by Rifle and M.G. fire. The raiding party made no attempt to work its way along the trenches but simply jumped in and dragged away the N.C.O. 2 hostile Rainforce Minenwerfers and Entwurfen but were dropped by the raiders. General trench repairs were carried out.	Rpt Ptd
	30		Enemy fairly quiet during the day until Hee exploded a mine in front of "C" Coy. The mine lip being about 20 yards from our front line. Considerable damage was done to our parapet and S.P.	
	1		14. Several men were buried as the result of the explosion but only one killed. Following the explosion we immediately sent forward Bombing Parties to occupy the near lip. No signs of the enemy	

WAR DIARY
or
INTELLIGENCE SUMMARY.
(Erase heading not required.)

Army Form C. 2118.

Place	Date	Hour	Summary of Events and Information	Remarks and references to Appendices
CUINCHY	30		was seen. At about 9 P.M. 2ND LIEUT. A.S. FABIAN took out a party to recover the body of a dead German seen lying in front of our trenches, evidently killed as the result of last night's raid. The patrol not only succeeded in recovering the German's Body but also that of the N.C.O. Capt. wired by the enemy. Both were dead. The German was from a SAXON REGT. He had removed all identification except his shd. cockades and Badges of rank. He wore a W.O.	
	31		During the day the enemy were very quiet, with the exception of sending over a few Whizz Bangs. Night was very quiet. Our T.M.Bs. were active in the evening, numerous Several direct hits in the enemy parapet. General trench maintenance and repairing damage done.	PRS

S. Hughes Capt
Commanding 13" Bn. R. Fus. R.,

116th Brigade.
39th Division.

13th BATTALION

THE ROYAL SUSSEX REGIMENT

JUNE 1916

Army Form C. 2118.

WAR DIARY
or
INTELLIGENCE SUMMARY.
(Erase heading not required.)

3/13 R Sussex Regt

Vol 4

Place	Date	Hour	Summary of Events and Information	Remarks and references to Appendices
Cinchy	1.6.16		The Battalion was relieved in the left sub-sector by the 11th Royal Sussex Regt. The relief commenced at 2:30 pm and was complete by 5:15 pm. The billets vacated by 11th Royal Sussex Regt were taken over and the following dispositions made:— A Company in Cambrin Point. B Company at Braddell Castle. C Company, 2 platoons at Crinchy Keep, 1 platoon in Carter's Post and 1 platoon at Tournbrexis. During the night of the 1st — 2nd 6.16 2nd Lt N.d.P. McRoberts carried out a reconnaissance of the enemy's wire in front of the North Post Loopstack. Bombs were thrown at our patrol without effect and the following observations were recorded. Enemy wire generally speaking thin, and the patrol found little difficulty in cutting it. One sentry was observed but no movement was heard in the enemy's line, and after observing for some considerable time the patrol withdrew quietly after having obtained the idea of obtaining information as to the strength of the troops in the enemy's wire which had been made with working parties.	D.4
	2.6.16		Battalion in support. Trench maintenance and working parties.	

Army Form C. 2118.

WAR DIARY
or
INTELLIGENCE SUMMARY.
(Erase heading not required.)

Instructions regarding War Diaries and Intelligence Summaries are contained in F. S. Regs., Part II. and the Staff Manual respectively. Title pages will be prepared in manuscript.

Place	Date	Hour	Summary of Events and Information	Remarks and references to Appendices
CUINCHY	2.6.16		The Battalion in support as previously stated. Trench working parties and maintenance continued throughout the day and night.	
	3.6.16		Trench maintenance as above.	
	4.6.16		Hostile artillery very active throughout the day and night. Enemy support Paul heavily shelled with whiz bangs and 4.2" guns. Considerable damage caused to the trenches but no casualties.	WC
	5.6.6		The 13th Bn Royal Sussex Reg. relieved the 11th R Sussex in the left sub-sector in the front line the following alterations were made to the front line. A Company took over the right company frontage in place of B. D Company the centre in place of C. B Company the left in place of A with C company in support Caporando Terrace. All companies reported the relief complete by 11.15. a.m. During the night an attempted raid under 2nd Lt. N.U.P. MacRobert's opposite the centre company succeeded in cutting through the enemy's wire to within fifteen feet of his parapet. Owing to the approach of dawn they were unable to complete the work and returned to our	PM

Army Form C. 2118.

WAR DIARY
or
INTELLIGENCE SUMMARY.
(Erase heading not required.)

Instructions regarding War Diaries and Intelligence Summaries are contained in F. S. Regs., Part II. and the Staff Manual respectively. Title pages will be prepared in manuscript.

Place	Date	Hour	Summary of Events and Information	Remarks and references to Appendices
CUINCHY	5.6.16		trenches without any casualties. Two hostile sentries were observed in the enemy's trenches but apparently neither of them observed our party while the wire was being cut. Our Lewis guns fired indirect throughout the night to cover the operations, otherwise the night was very quiet, and there was less rifle and machine gun fire than usual. Commendable coolness was displayed by all the men, and the silence with which the wire was cut spoke very highly for the keenness and efficiency of the parties engaged.	
	6.6.16		Very little artillery activity in the morning. The enemy fired twelve 4.2" shells at N° 11 breastwork at 1.30 p.m. Our artillery replied, and the enemy ceased fire. Rainfall fairly heavy during the night. Weather improved in the afternoon. At about 11.45 p.m. the raid which had been planned for the previous night was again entered attempted this time with more success. 2nd Lt McRoberts and 36 other ranks left our trenches at A 16 c 40 55 and advanced up to the German wire accompanied by an engineer officer and two sappers with a bangalore torpedo. The latter was placed	

Army Form C. 2118.

WAR DIARY
or
INTELLIGENCE SUMMARY.
(Erase heading not required.)

Instructions regarding War Diaries and Intelligence Summaries are contained in F. S. Regs., Part II. and the Staff Manual respectively. Title pages will be prepared in manuscript.

Place	Date	Hour	Summary of Events and Information	Remarks and references to Appendices
CUINCHY	6.6.16		in gap which had been made the previous night and the Sappers returned to our front line trenches. At 12.5.a.m the message was received that all was ready and the F.O.O phoned back to the Artillery to stand by. After a slight pause the torpedo was fired electrically from the front line and simultaneously the Artillery opened fir. Immediately the explosion had taken place the officer and parties rushed through the gap. Unfortunately it is believed that the enemy were not entirely surprised from the fact that a barrage of bombs was thrown out in front having the effect of cutting off Lt McRobert from his leading party. He however entered the German trench and ran over two dead bodies, and after a struggle with an enemy sentry was wounded in the hand and head. In the meantime the second parties reached the trench and were greeted with a shower of bombs from the enemy who appeared to be fairly strong. They however bombed along the top of the parapet inflicting considerable casualties on the enemy. Lt McRobert then gave the order to "man off" and the parties made their way back independently to our trench. Our casualties amounted to 1 officer	W.C.

T2134. Wt. W708—776. 500000. 4/15. Sir J. C. & S.

Army Form C. 2118.

WAR DIARY
or
INTELLIGENCE SUMMARY.
(Erase heading not required.)

Instructions regarding War Diaries and Intelligence Summaries are contained in F. S. Regs., Part II. and the Staff Manual respectively. Title pages will be prepared in manuscript.

Place	Date	Hour	Summary of Events and Information	Remarks and references to Appendices
CUINCHY	6.6.16		and 14 O.R. wounded, none of them seriously. Great credit was due to 2nd Lt. M. of P. McTolock for the success of the operation, and also to the other officer for his valuable assistance with the torpedo.	MC
	7.6.16		At about 2.p.m. the enemy fired a few whizz bangs on the left company frontage without doing any damage. Otherwise the day was quiet. During the night our machine guns were active particularly in the spot where the raid of the previous night took place. The enemy apparently made no attempt to repair the damage done.	MC
	8.6.16		The batt was relieved in the left sub-sector by the 11th R. Sussex taking over the billets evacuated by the 11th at Annequin north. The relief was completed by 12.45 p.m.	MC
	9.6.16		The day was devoted to billet cleaning and maintenance. P.E. working parties were supplied.	MC
	10.6.16		The batt was relieved by the 1/4th Suffolks and moved back to Divisional reserve in billets about La Pannerie.	MC
LA PANNERIE	11.6.16		Parade according to Brigade training programme.	MC

T.134. Wt. W708—776. 500000. 4/15. Sir J. C. & S.

Army Form C. 2118.

WAR DIARY
or
INTELLIGENCE SUMMARY.
(Erase heading not required.)

Instructions regarding War Diaries and Intelligence Summaries are contained in F.S. Regs., Part II. and the Staff Manual respectively. Title pages will be prepared in manuscript.

Place	Date	Hour	Summary of Events and Information	Remarks and references to Appendices
LA PANNERIE	12.6.16		The Commanding Officer inspected the kits of the battalion and noted for the necessary articles forwarded to the Qms.	
	13.6.16		The companies paraded on the divisional digging ground near Locon continuing with the trenches which were commenced on the 25th May 1916. Weather became very cold and wet and the men returned to billets about 2 p.m.	
	14.6.16		Company Commanders went on a tour of the trenches in the Ferme du Bois section, preparatory to the Division taking over a new frontage.	
	15.6.16		Companies carried out rapid and application practices on the small range near headquarters. Major Bellamy having reported for duty was taken on the strength of the battalion and assumed second in command.	
	16.6.16		The battalion relieved the 17th Lanc. Fusiliers in the Ferme du Bois section its following dispositions being made. Three companies in the front line and one in support. A coy on the night, C company in the centre, D coy. on the left and B coy. in support at Bull Street. The battalion left billets at La Pannerie at 5.45 p.m and guides from	

Army Form C. 2118.

WAR DIARY
or
INTELLIGENCE SUMMARY.
(Erase heading not required.)

Instructions regarding War Diaries and Intelligence Summaries are contained in F. S. Regs., Part II. and the Staff Manual respectively. Title pages will be prepared in manuscript.

Place	Date	Hour	Summary of Events and Information	Remarks and references to Appendices
	16.6.16		The Lancs. Fusiliers at Richebourg St. Vaast at 8.30 p.m. All coys reported relief complete at 10.55 p.m. The relief was completed without a casualty. Battalion H.Qrs. [S.9.a.6½.5] Bethune Combined sheet.	
Ferme du Bois	17.6.16		With the exception of dropping a few "Minnies" on the head of Plum Street at about 6.30 p.m the enemy was very quiet. There was the usual machine gun & rifle activity during the night. Our trench mortars registered onto enemy trench in the afternoon. The usual patrols reconnoitred during the night. During one of these patrols, Capt Gillespie & Lt Rigby were both wounded, the former seriously and the latter only slightly. Enemy very quiet except for machine gun and rifle fire at nights.	※
"	18.6.16		Our rifle grenade went adrift both during the day and nights. Captain F.S. Gillespie reported died of wounds. This was a great blow to the battalion and one very much felt by all ranks. This officer was a model of energy and cheerfulness in the performance of his duty, and was always ready to help anyone who was in trouble. His funeral took place at Merville and was attended by 2nd Lt Jones and 2nd Lt M Sparks, 2nd Lt Dickens	

Army Form C. 2118.

WAR DIARY
or
INTELLIGENCE SUMMARY.
(Erase heading not required.)

Instructions regarding War Diaries and Intelligence Summaries are contained in F. S. Regs., Part II. and the Staff Manual respectively. Title pages will be prepared in manuscript.

Place	Date	Hour	Summary of Events and Information	Remarks and references to Appendices
FERME DU BOIS	18.6.16		Captain R.D'A Whittaker reported to this battalion for duty and was posted to D Company. Captain R.D'A Whittaker temporarily took on command of D Company and Lt. H.J. Coxhead was appointed adjutant.	
	19.6.16		The enemy dropped a few whizz bangs near Cadburys- Cockspur St slightly damaging the trench but causing no casualties. Slight interchange of bombs at Boar's head sap. During the night our Lewis guns dispersed a hostile wiring party. Weather rather cold, wind south-west, about three miles an hour.	
	20.6.16		Enemy bombarded our line at intervals during the day only doing slight damage and wounding one man slightly. Machine guns were active during the night and there was a certain amount of bombing activity in the Boars head sap during which Lt. E.V. Clarke was wounded in the leg and thigh, but not seriously. Patrols under Captn Whittaker, 2nd Lt. Whitley, 2nd Lt Prior went out during the day and night into No. man's land. Direction of wind west about 5 miles per hour. Weather much warmer.	

Army Form C. 2118.

WAR DIARY
or
INTELLIGENCE SUMMARY.
(Erase heading not required.)

Instructions regarding War Diaries and Intelligence Summaries are contained in F.S. Regs., Part II. and the Staff Manual respectively. Title pages will be prepared in manuscript.

Place	Date	Hour	Summary of Events and Information	Remarks and references to Appendices
FERME DU BOIS	21.6.16		The enemy artillery was active during the day, shelling our trenches and also Windy Corner. A few casualties amongst a bathing party of B. Company were sustained. Our rifle grenades were again active with visibly good results. The Battalion was relieved in the trenches by the 14th Bn. Hampshires taking over the following posts and billets evacuated by the relieving battalion. A Company :- Cole Post 3.15.A.6.5½. Orchard Post S.14.b.5.8. Oblong Post S.8.d.5.4. Days Post S.9.c.2.½. Scott S.8.a.2.0. Hunter S.8.a.2.3. Billets [S.8.a.7.9. S.8.b.1.4.] H.Q's S.8.b.3½.3. B. Coy. Edwards Post S.9.a.8.9. Hens S.3.d.1.3. Rags S.2.c.9.9. Bones S.2.b.1.0. H.Q. S.8.a.7.9. C. Coy. Billets S.2.a.2.7. D. Coy. [9oRs & Argls] S.2.a.8.8. St. Vaast R.32.d.7.2. Richebourg S.2.c.3.1. Companies reported relief complete 3.15. a.m.	※
	22.6.16		The battalion was relieved by the 11th Herts regiment, moving to billets at Vieille Chapelle, evacuated by the relieving battalion. Companies reported all in billets at 11.45 p.m.	
	23.6.16		The Battalion remained under the G.O.C. 116th Inf. Bn. for administration, discipline and training, but otherwise temporarily formed part of Brigade in Divisional Reserve. The officers of the battalion were informed of a future operation to be carried out	※

T.1134. Wt. W708—776. 500000. 4/15. Sir J. C. & S.

Army Form C. 2118.

WAR DIARY
or
INTELLIGENCE SUMMARY.
(Erase heading not required.)

Instructions regarding War Diaries and Intelligence Summaries are contained in F. S. Regs., Part II. and the Staff Manual respectively. Title pages will be prepared in manuscript.

Place	Date	Hour	Summary of Events and Information	Remarks and references to Appendices
VIEILLE CHAPELLE	23.6.16		by the Brigadier and the plans of action were discussed. The Corps Commander presented the Medal Ribbons to Ptes Parvin, Ford, and Balcombe. Weather very warm sharp thunderstorm about 4.30 p.m.	
	24.6.16		The morning was devoted to interior economy, and fifty men from each company had a talk. In the afternoon the Bn. marched to the Divisional training ground [B.19.C] to practise carrying out the attack companies marched off independently at 2 p.m.	
	25.6.16		Companies marched off independently to the training ground for attack practice. Special bombing squads under 2nd Lt Ellis marched to the 35th Divisional bombing ground at LE PACAUT (Q.23.a.3.6).	
	26.6.16		Companies paraded at 9 a.m and marched to the 35th Div" training ground LE PACAUT (Q.23.a.3.6) and practised the attack on the new trenches returning in the afternoon to the training ground at [R.19.d].	
	27.6.16		Weather very wet training abandoned owing to rain. In the afternoon companies detailed 50 men for the baths .. clean change of clothing issued out.	
FERME DU BOIS	28.6.16		Bn. relieved the 14th Bn Hants in the right sub sector, FERME DU BOIS	

Army Form C. 2118.

WAR DIARY
or
INTELLIGENCE SUMMARY.
(Erase heading not required.)

Instructions regarding War Diaries and Intelligence Summaries are contained in F. S. Regs., Part II. and the Staff Manual respectively. Title pages will be prepared in manuscript.

Place	Date	Hour	Summary of Events and Information	Remarks and references to Appendices
FERME DU BOIS	28.6.16		and moved to the following billets: B and C companies in the front line, A in Richebourg St Vaast Post, and D in billets VIEILLE CHAPELLE	
	29.6.16		Day spent in collecting materials and general organization for the attack. In the afternoon our artillery bombarded the enemy trenches from 2 p.m. to 5 p.m. cutting his wire and destroying his works. A copy of operation order No. 25 is attached.	
	30.6.16		Report on Operations.	
		1	The Battalion assembled at 1.30 p.m. on the morning of the 30th June in readiness for the assault with all four platoons of each coy in the front line.	
		2	The preliminary bombardment on the morning of the attack opened at 2.50 a.m. and at 3.5 the leading wave of the battalion scaled the parapet the remainder followed at 50 yds interval. At the same time the front attack under its Lt. Coly. and this game afiring in its swing trench. The passage across No Man's Land was accomplished with few casualties in except in the left companies which came under a very heavy machine gun fire. The two right companies succeeded in reaching their objective but the two left companies only succeeded in penetrating the enemy line in one or two places.	

T.J.134. Wt. W708-776. 500000. 4/15. Sir J.C. & S.

Army Form C. 2118.

WAR DIARY
or
INTELLIGENCE SUMMARY.
(Erase heading not required.)

Instructions regarding War Diaries and Intelligence Summaries are contained in F. S. Regs., Part II. and the Staff Manual respectively. Title pages will be prepared in manuscript.

Place	Date	Hour	Summary of Events and Information	Remarks and references to Appendices
FERME DU BOIS	29.6.16		Just at this moment a smoke cloud which had originally delayed to mask our advance drifted right across the front and made it impossible to see more than a few yards ahead. This resulted in all direction being lost and the attack drifting into small bodies of men not knowing which way to go. Some groups succeeded in entering the support line engaging the enemy with bombs and bayonet and organizing to hold stages of a defence. Other parties swung off to the right and entered the French when the flank party was operating, causing a great deal of congestion. On the left the smoke and darkness made the job of penetrating the enemy won so difficult that few if any succeeded in reaching the enemy trench. Some parties of the right company succeeded in reaching the enemy support line when they were subjected to an intense bombardment with H.E and whizz bangs. Capt. Hughes who was wounded seeing that the Coy. was in danger of being cut off, gave the order for the succession of the enemy trenches and the remainder of the attackers force returned to our trenches. The enemy who was evidently thoroughly prepared now concentrated his energies on its front line and for the space of about 2½ hours our front and support line were subjected to an intense bombardment with heavy and light shells causing a large	

Army Form C. 2118.

WAR DIARY
or
INTELLIGENCE SUMMARY.
(Erase heading not required.)

Instructions regarding War Diaries and Intelligence Summaries are contained in F. S. Regs., Part II. and the Staff Manual respectively. Title pages will be prepared in manuscript.

Place	Date	Hour	Summary of Events and Information	Remarks and references to Appendices
FERME DU BOIS	30.6.14		number of casualties. Ultimately the shelling ceased and it is all likely and perhaps the operations closed. The battn being relieved by the 14th Hants at about 1.30 p.m. and taking over their original billets at VIEILLE CHAPELLE.	
			Principal causes of failure.	
			a) The unfortunate incident of the smoke cloud.	
			b) The preparedness of the enemy.	
			c) The intensity of the enemy's shell and machine gun fire.	
			d) The failure of the Artillery to cut the enemy's wire on the left.	
			Casualties. Our casualties were unfortunately heavy and resulted in the loss of many valuable Officers and men including Capt. An Humble-Crofts, Capt. & Adj. R.D.A. Wittich, Lt Fitzherbert M.L.A? Lt Dudley Morgan, Lieuts Frost A.L. and Diggens (killed and missing) and Capt Hughes, Capt Wakelam, Lt W.W. Fitzherbert, 2nd Lt Turner wounded. Amongst the wounded were C.S.M. Robinson, C.S.M. Juneo, C.S.M Sears and C.S.M. Hadfry, the latter lost a foot during the bombardment. The enemy casualties were also considered to have been considerable. Large numbers of dead being seen in the enemy's trenches.	

COPY No. 8.

OPERATION ORDER No 23

INTENTION
1) The Battalion will assault and capture the enemy trenches as follows :-
   a) Enemy front line from BOARS HEAD to S.10.c.8.1
   b) Enemy support line from S.10.c.5½.6½ to S.10.c.9.9

   The 12th Battalion will assault on our left.
   The dividing line between the Battalions will be the ditch running from our front line parapet at S.10.c.5.3 to the enemy front line parapet at S.10.c.8.0

METHOD OF ATTACK
2)
   a) Main Attack from our front line between CINDER TRACK [S.10.c.0.2] and the ditch [S.10.c.5.3] near VINE STREET.
   b) Flank Attack from our own FISHTAIL SAP against the BOARS HEAD.

   i) Main attack will be delivered in 4 lines, each line consisting of 4 platoons - i.e. one from each company in single rank - with one pace extensions.
   ii) Flank attack will be delivered by 5 bombing parties each party consisting of 1 N.C.O. and 5 men.

ASSEMBLY FOR ASSAULT

MAIN ATTACK

The platoons from each company forming the 1st line of assault will assemble in front line Russian Saps 54-55 inclusive.
A Coy on the right, then from right to left B - C - D Coys.
The platoons forming the 2nd line of assault will assemble in the new salient trench.
These, for the second line, in the rear bays.
The two platoons forming the 3rd & 4th lines from each company will assemble in the old support trench between CINDER TRACK and VINE STREET.
A Company on the right, then from right to left B - C - D Coys in rear of their platoons of their own coys forming the 1st & 2nd lines.
The platoons of each company detailed for the 3rd line will be on the right of those detailed for the 4th line.

FLANK ATTACK

The parties detailed for the flank attack will assemble in our front line between the junction with FISHTAIL SAP. The sap in front of our front line and support line will be cut. Further company arrangements the night previous to the assault.

LEWIS GUNS

These will assemble in the old assembly trench about 55 yards in front of trench between BOND STREET and VINE STREET

2.

2nd Lt ELPHICKE
RSM CHANCE
NCO 20
8 men from each
Coy.

CARRYING PARTY will assemble in the STRAND

As soon as the assaulting troops have advanced over the front parapet these parties will move to the enemy lines situated on our present front line. Their duty will be to transfer S.A.A. - Bombs - Rations and water from the stores to the companies situated in the new front line.
Silence must be insisted on.

[left margin: OBJECT OF THE ASSAULT]

At .... precisely the Artillery will begin to lift from the first line. Until then the parapet... for the enemy trench the platoons of the assault line will follow at a distance of 50 yards.
The objective of the first three lines will be the enemy's second line from S.16.a.5½.6½ to S.16.a.5.0.
They will on no account halt in the enemy's front line but push on to the enemy's support lines.

As soon as the second line has cleared our front line parapet, the third will advance afrom the Support trench climb over the parapet & follow the other lines...
The fourth line will act in a similar manner.
The distances between lines throughout should be 50 yards
The objective of the 4th line will be the enemy's present front line.
The left of each line with officers and each platoon will be approximately on a frontage of 50 yards.

If possible every effort will be made...before the appointed hour is... advance... our front parapet. In that case the third and fourth lines will... keep... 50 yards...
front parapet.

...

FLANK ATTACK

[left margin:
2nd Lt ELGG
2 Lt WHITLEY
NCO 28 bombs
A Coy
B Coy
C Coy
D Coy
NCO 18
Bullets & bombs
4 snipers.]

at .... when the Artillery lifts this parties will ...enemy trench... for the enemy supp... either his front line trench at the BOAR'S HEAD
They will bomb enemy front line trench from N.2
Communication trench to its left blocking enemy front line trench beyond position.
This will be carried by rifle bombing party ... They will blow on the parapet to mark...

LEWIS GUNS

As soon as the infantry advance commences the Lewis guns will open fire on the enemy parapet.
... field of fire to be cleared by...
Troops, they will advance to ... and ... yards from our parapet.

BLOCKING PARTIES

When a position has been secured in the enemy support line, blocking parties are detailed off. H ot enemy communication trenches at points O @ & as shewn on accompanying map.

A sapper with explosive will accompany each party.

DUG OUT PARTIES

Special bombing parties will accompany each platoon in 1st line. These parties will enter enemy front lines & bomb all dug outs to prevent our leading lines being bombed from behind. They will work from right to left.

Bombing Parties will be detailed as follows —

A Coy to enter trench at V
& bomb to point Q

B Coy to bomb trench P as far as Q
then push on to point line

C Coy to bomb up trench R to point X
& then to point Q

D Coy to bomb up trench S then to X
& then bomb trench to K

These parties will accompany our 1st assembling line.

CONSOLIDATION OF POSITION

5] Assoon as the position is secured it will be consolidated again at once against a possible counter attack. To effect this the RE will erect strong points at A B & C as shewn on accompanying map.

The intervening trench will be consolidated by the assaulting infantry (1st & 2nd lines)

New breastworks 100 Yards / knock will be constructed by a pioneer battalion who will also construct the following new communication trenches — on the LEFT feature COPSE ST CENTRE VINE ST RIGHT BOND ST

[illegible lines]

On no account is "straggling or souvenir hunting to be allowed.

The new front line will be consolidated by the 1st & 23rd lines
The NEW support line will be consolidated by the new trench

DETAIL OF TOOLS
Bombs, Ammunition to be carried

6]
220 rounds of SAA will be issued to each man with the exception of the bombers.

Sandbags will be carried as follows —

Each man in the 1st line will carry one sandbag
" " " 2nd " " " two "
" " " 3rd " " " four "

"4"

Tools will be carried as follows:—

1 pick or shovel to every man in 2nd line
1   do   do   do 3rd line
1   do   do   do 4th line

Bombs Bombers will carry 12 bombs
All other men will carry two bombs each as a reserve for company bombers.
Platoon commanders will arrange to collect these as a platoon reserve. It must be distinctly understood that only trained bombers are to use these bombs.

Rations Each man will carry two days rations and will start with a full water bottle.
O.C Companies will hold an inspection of iron rations a day or so previous to the assault.

Packs will be collected and dumped in a spot to be notified later. Each man will carry a waterproof sheet to be fixed to the back of his belt.

Gas Helmets
All gas helmets MUST be examined by Company Officers.

7] **Reserve SAA** is distributed along our front line parapet and at the head of the following communication trenches
CONNAUGHT STREET
COCKSPUR STREET
BOND STREET
VINE STREET

Bombs will be distributed as follows:—

<u>First Reserve</u>
Front parapet near FISH TAIL   2,000
Head of COCKSPUR STREET   1,600
  "   BOND STREET   1,600

<u>2nd Reserve Store</u> Junction of BOND STREET & GUARDS 6,000

<u>3rd Reserve Store</u> In ORCHARD about the COPSE   6,000

RE Stores
Dumps will be established as under
A] FISH TAIL behind the parapet forward end of VINE STREET
B]

5.

RATIONS AND WATER

Stores of water and rations will be established at the forward end of the following Communication Trenches

    CONNAUGHT STREET
    COCKSPUR STREET
    BOND STREET
    VINE STREET

8] O.C. Companies will make the following arrangements as soon as the enemy position has been captured

  I] Collect all tools found in enemy trenches
  II] Latrine accomodation
  III] Whether water is available if so it should be tasted and protected
  IV] Selected sites for Company stores i.e. S.A.A. Grenades water etc.

BATTALION SNIPERS

Will advance on flanks of third line
Special instructions will be issued to sniping sergeant.

EVACUATION OF WOUNDED

All wounded men will be evacuated to the Regimental Aid Post VIA — COCKSPUR STREET — RUE de BOIS — to EDWARD STREET.

9] Reports to Advanced Battalion Headquarters in BOND STREET

Copy No. 1 To O.C. A Coy
    2 To O.C. B Coy
    3 To O.C. C Coy
    4 To O.C. D Coy
    5 To M.G. Officer
    6 To 2nd in Command
    7 To C.O.
    8 To War Diary
    9 To Bombing Officer

26/6/16

H.W. Daffarn Col.
Comdg 9th Royal Sussex Regt

SECRET — Appendix A — Copy No.

Communications

1. The Battalion Advanced Report Centre is in a shelter off BOND STREET Communication trench.

   There is telephonic communication with Advance Brigade Report Centre, with Centre Battalion Report Centre in VINE STREET, and with Left Battalion Advanced Report Centre in COPSE STREET.

2. A line has been laid from Right Battalion Report Centre to our present front line trench at S.10.c.3.1½. This line will be continued along main ditch to point S.16.a.5.8½ in enemy trench in part which will be occupied by rear platoon of B. Co. A line has been laid from Centre Battalion Report Centre to our present front line trench at S.10.c.5.3. The line will be continued along ditch to point S.16.a.7½.0 in enemy trench in part to be occupied by rear platoon of D Co.

   Visual Signalling by means of discs and Electric signalling lamp will be also established between these two stations and an observation post at FACTORY.

3. 18 pigeons are available each day. They must always be sent in pairs and each message duplicated.

   This will only give 9 complete messages, therefore pigeons must not be used until everything else has failed.

4. Runners must be informed of nearest signal office (they will all be marked by Notice Boards) and instructed to call there before going on. It is most important that all ranks should be informed of these positions.

   All messages sent by runners must be duplicated and sent by different routes.

SECRET   Woodtest Op. No 8

Appendix B

1. On the night of the 28th inst. the Battalion will take over the right sub-sector, as follows:—

    from CADBURYS to BOND STREET (inclusive)

    The dividing line between the 13th and 12th Battalions will be BOND STREET (inclusive to 13th Batt) and a line drawn in prolongation of BOND STREET in a NORTH WEST direction.

    The disposition of the Battalion will be as follows:—

    In front immediate support line   B & C Cos

    In reserve trench
        (PALL MALL, & part of RIGHT GUARDS) ½ D Co

    In Bullets behind Batt. Headquarters A Co

    Battalion Headquarters   BOND STREET
                                          (with use of house @ S.q.a.8.5)

2. A few hours preceding the assault the Battalion will assemble in the position described in para. 2 of Battalion Operation Order No 23.

3. The positions vacated, i.e. CADBURYS to COCKSPUR STREET in front line, PALL MALL and part of RIGHT GUARDS will be occupied by 2 Cos of 14th HANTS.

3. As our assaulting columns leave our front line, their place will be taken by 1 Co. of 14th HANTS.

SECRET

OPERATION ORDER
No. 25

A 69 to 76
(inclusive)
B 77 to 86
C 87 to 93
D 94 to 3
(inclusive)

1. The Battalion will assemble for the assault as follows during the night of the 29th / 30th June

   A Co. will move from RICHEBOURG ST VAAST via WINDY CORNER EDWARDS ROAD - COCKSPUR STREET to trenches passing Battalion Headquarters at 11 p.m. At Battalion Headquarters each man will be issued with an extra 100 rounds of ammunition and 2 bombs, also sandbags. A Co., will enter front line trenches via COCKSPUR STREET and will assemble with 2 platoons in support trench Bays 69 to 76 (inclusive) and 2 platoons in support trench immediately behind.

   B Co., will be relieved by A Co., 14th HANTS which will reach junction of CADBURYS and Front Line Trench at 12 midnight. B Co. will then assemble with 2 platoons in Bays 77 to 86 inclusive and 2 platoons in Support Trench immediately behind.

   C Co., will be assembled with 2 platoons in Bays 87 to 93 inclusive by 12 midnight, with 2 platoons in Support Trench immediately behind.
   THE FISH TAIL SAP will not however be evacuated until taken over by 14th HANTS.

   D Co., will leave present billets and move via WINDY CORNER (S.9.a.6.9½) - Battalion Headquarters (S.9.a.6½ & VINE STREET and will assemble with 2 platoons in Bays 94 to 3 (inclusive), and 2 platoons in Support Line immediately behind.
   Head of D Co., to pass Battalion Headquarters at 11.45 p.m. At Battalion Headquarters each man will be issued with an extra 100 rounds of ammunition and 2 bombs, also sandbags.

   LEWIS GUNS will assemble as already detailed by 1 a.m. 30th June.

   NOTE - O.C., Cos may, at their discretion, assemble 3 platoons in Front Line instead of 2, owing to the extremely wet and muddy state of Support Trenches.

FLANK ATTACK   Bombing Squads as already detailed.)
               10 carriers to be detailed by   ) Will assemble at
               2/ Lieut ELPHICKE   ) Headquarters
               Pte Young B Co.,   ) (S.9.a.6.5) at
               Pte Astridge A Co.,   ) 9 p.m. and report
               3 Sappers   ) to 2/Lieut ELLIS

CARRYING PARTY The carrying party as already detailed will report to 2/Lieut ELPHICKE at Battalion Headquarters (S.9.a.6.5)

REPORT   at 10 p.m. tonight (29th)
                Battalion Headquarters will move to BOND STREET at

WIRE   12 midnight.
                In front of both Support and Front Line Trench will be out under Company arrangements.

BRIDGES   Special Bridges have been made in Brigade Workshops, and will be put out by O.C., Brigade Workshops (Capt FINAY) in front of our trenches. Other Bridges are in the line and will be put out by O.C., Cos.,

                          (sgd) H.J.COXHEAD
                                    Lieut - Adjutant.

SECRET   OPERATION ORDER
                          No. 25

A 69 to 76   1. The Battalion will assemble for the assault as follows
  (inclusive)   during the night of the 29th / 30th June
B 77 to 86   A Co. will move from RICHEBOURG ST VAAST via WINDY CORNER
C 87 to 93   EDWARDS ROAD - COCKSPUR STREET to trenches passing
D 94 to 3   Battalion Headquarters at 11 p.m. At Battalion
  (inclusive)   Headquarters each man will be issued with an extra 100
                   rounds of ammunition and 2 bombs, also sandbags. A Co.,
                   will enter front line trenches via COCKSPUR STREET and
                   will assemble with 2 platoons in support trench Bays
                   69 to 76 (inclusive) and 2 platoons in support trench
                   immediately behind.
                   B Co., will be relieved by A Co., 14th HANTS which will
                   reach junction of CADBURYS and Front Line Trench at
                   12 midnight. B Co. will then assemble with 2 platoons
                   in Bays 77 to 86 inclusive and 2 platoons in Support
                   Trench immediately behind.
                   C Co., will be assembled with 2 platoons in Bays 87 to 93
                   inclusive by 12 midnight, with 2 platoons in Support
                   Trench immediately behind.
                     THE FISH TAIL SAP will not however be evacuated
                   until taken over by 14th HANTS.
                   D Co., will leave present billets and move via WINDY
                   CORNER (S.9.a.6.9½) - Battalion Headquarters (S.9.a.8.5)
                   VINE STREET and will assemble with 2 platoons in Bays
                   94 to 3 (inclusive), and 2 platoons in Support Line
                   immediately behind.
                     Head of D Co., to pass Battalion Headquarters at
                   11.45 p.m. At Battalion Headquarters each man will
                   be issued with an extra 100 rounds of ammunition and
                   2 bombs, also sandbags.
                   LEWIS GUNS will assemble as already detailed by 1 a.m.
                   30th June

                   NOTE - O.C., Cos may, at their discretion, assemble 3
                       platoons in Front Line instead of 2, owing to the
                       extremely wet and muddy state of Support Trenches.

FLANK ATTACK   Bombing Squads as already detailed.) Will assemble at
                10 carriers to be detailed by   ) Headquarters
                2/ Lieut ELPHICKE   ) (S.9.a.8.5) at
                Pte Young B Co.,   ) 9 p.m. and report
                Pte Astridge A Co.,   ) to 2/Lieut ELLIS
                3 Sappers   )
CARRYING PARTY The carrying party as already detailed will report to
                2/Lieut ELPHICKE at Battalion Headquarters (S.9.a.8.5)
                at 10 p.m. tonight (29th)
REPORT   Battalion Headquarters will move to BOND STREET at
                12 midnight.
WIRE   In front of both Support and Front Line Trench will be
                cut under Company arrangements.
BRIDGES   Special Bridges have been made in Brigade Workshops, and
                will be put out by O.C., Brigade Workshops (Capt FINLAY)
                in front of our trenches. Other Bridges are in the line
                and will be put out by O.C., Cos.
                            (sgd) H.J.COXHEAD
                                  Lieut -a/Adjutant.

116th Brigade.
39th Division.

13th BATTALION

THE ROYAL SUSSEX REGIMENT

JULY   1 9 1 6

39/vol 5

D.5

Confidential

War Diary
of
13th Bn R.Sussex R.
from July 1st 1916 to 31st July 1916.

Army Form C. 2118.

WAR DIARY
or
INTELLIGENCE SUMMARY.
(Erase heading not required.)

Place	Date	Hour	Summary of Events and Information	Remarks and references to Appendices
VIEILLE CHAPELLE	1.7.16.		Battn in billets at Vieille Chapelle - west of reorganization commenced. Gaps allotted to the Coys.	
	2.7.16.		Major Bellamy D.S.O. temporarily appointed in command of the 12th R. Sussex vice Col. Impey wounded.	
	3.7.16.		Bn in billets. The C. O. Commander addressed the Bn on the lastest field. VIEILLE CHAPELLE LACOUTURE ROAD Training programme commenced. Capt. W.T. Heagarty returned to duty after attending Assistant Staff Captain 116th Inf. Bde. and was appointed O.C. B Coy. v. 4.7.16. 2nd Lt Cushman reported for duty and was posted to B Coy.	
	4.7.16.		Bn in billets. Training of bombers, signallers, machine gunners + snipers.	
BETHUNE	5.7.16.		The Bn moved to billets in BETHUNE. Batt. paraded at 10 p.m. outside Coy billets and marched via the LOCON-BETHUNE road to billets at 208 de Jeunes filles. All in billets and to the Brigade 12.35 a.m.	
	6.7.16.		Capt. W. Heagarty relinquished command of B Coy and resumed the duties of acting second in command of the Bn. late 7.7.16. At 9hs resumed command of B Coy. date 7.7.16. The Bn relieved the 2nd A & S Highlanders at Annequin South. Bn marched by the main BETHUNE - LA BASSEE ROAD by half companies at 200 yds interval. Relief reported complete by companies at 10.45 p.m.	
	7.7.16.			

WAR DIARY
or
INTELLIGENCE SUMMARY.
(Erase heading not required.)

Army Form C. 2118.

Place	Date	Hour	Summary of Events and Information	Remarks and references to Appendices
ANNEQUIN SOUTH	8.7.16		Battalion has to furnish heavy working parties for 251st Coy RE at No 11 Brickstack and CAMERON SUPPORT POINT. HQ² Staff furnished parties.	HH
	9.7.16.		Enemy fires a few shells near the BETHUNE ANNEQUIN Cross Roads at about 11.45 pm. Bn supplied 186 men for 251st Coy RE working parties. Church service held in the courtyard outside Bn HQrs. Great deal of German and British aerial activity. One german machine brought down by our anti-aircraft guns.	HH
	10.7.16		Officers commanding companies reconnoitred the CUINCHY left sub section preparatory to taking over the line from the 14th Hampshires. The usual working parties were found by the Battn	HH
	11.7.16		The Battn relieved the left and left centre coys of the 14th in the CUINCHY SECTION this sector being temporarily called the left sub sector. A.& B. Coys joined together forming Nº 1 Coy and took over from the left centre coy of the 14th Hants and B & C formed Nº 2 Coy relieving the left coy of the 14th Hants. Coys reported relief complete at 8.45 a.m. A certain amount of trench mortar activity during the night. No damage done.	
CUINCHY	12.7.16		Heavy minenwerfer very active all day. considerable damage done to our trenches especially opposite start end in the neighborhood of the brickstacks. Sgt White of D coy.	

T.134. W⁺. W708-776. 500000. 4/15. Sir J. C. & S.

Army Form C. 2118.

WAR DIARY
or
INTELLIGENCE SUMMARY.
(Erase heading not required.)

Place	Date	Hour	Summary of Events and Information	Remarks and references to Appendices
CUINCHY	12.7.16		buried by a big "minnie". A party worked unceasingly to try and get him out but all hope had to be abandoned. Our artillery engaged the hostile trench mortar at intervals throughout the day and night but were unable to silence it. Four new officers arrived to the Bn. 2nd Lt. MacNaughton.A. 2nd Lt. Ward.O. 2nd Lt. Attwood.M. 2nd Lt 2nd Lt White and were posted to the A, C, B, D companies respectively.	
	13.7.16		The Bn. was relieved in the left and centre by A & B Coys of the 1st R. Hants moving to the Village line and CUINCHY SUPPORT posts. The following posts were taken over by the Companies:- A Coy. CHURCH KEEP, LEWIS KEEP, RAILWAY KEEP. B Coy. CAMBRIN SUPPORT POINT. CARTERS REDOUBT, TOURBIÈRES POST, CAMBRIN BOMB STORE. C Coy. CUINCHY SUPPORT POINT. MOUNTAIN KEEP, STAFFORD KEEP. D Coy. BRADDELL CASTLE, SIMMS KEEP, ARTHURS KEEP, RUSSEL KEEP. The enemy fired a large number of 4.2 shells onto BRADDELL CASTLE about 4.30 pm doing slight damage but causing no casualties.	
	14.7.16		The Bn. was relieved by the 2nd West Yorkshire regiment in the VILLAGE LINE and CUINCHY SUPPORT posts. Guides from each post met the parties of relieving Bn. at ANNEQUIN CROSS ROADS and led them to their respective posts. The last company reported relief complete at 2.35 a.m. The posts were relieved & independently marched to billets	

T.1134. Wt. W708-776. 500000. 4/15. Sir J. C. & S.

Army Form C. 2118.

WAR DIARY
or
INTELLIGENCE SUMMARY.
(Erase heading not required.)

Place	Date	Hour	Summary of Events and Information	Remarks and references to Appendices
LE TOURET	15.7.16		in LE TOURET. Lieut H.J. Corbet was appointed adjt. vice Capt. B.D. Whitaker missing. Authority XI Corps A.B/176 d.14.7.16. Four new officers reported to the Battalion :— 2nd Lt E.J. Ormsby, 2nd Lt H.I. Trigg, 2nd Lt. E.J. Harden, 2nd Lt F.W. Banner, 2nd Lt F.W. Custer posted to C — A — B — D coys. respectively. Coys sent a percentage of men to the baths.	M.K.
	16.7.16		Companies furnished a working party of 1 O.R. 5 N.C.Os 50 O.R. for the R.E. workshops BETHUNE near baths. at LES FACONS alloted to the battn. Church services for R.C.s & C. of E.s memorandums.	M.K.
	17.7.16		Company Training carried on under O.C. companies. B Coy passed through the gas chamber BEDLAM BUILDINGS (X.10.b.2.5). Bombers paraded for instruction under Lt. Ellis.	M.K.
	18.7.16		Company Training and specialist training carried on. "Under authority from the g.o.c in chief the Corps Commander awarded the military medal to the undermentioned N.C.Os & men for gallantry and devotion to duty in action:— No 2896 Pte C. Davies No 2819 Pte L. West No 3340 Pte Emsley No 5095 Pte Cooper F.A. No 2641 LCpl Chambers No 3521 Sergt. CE. Ball No 2693 LSgt. Harrold No 2947 LCpl Knight No 2854 Pte Bailey.	M.K.
	19.7.16		Company and specialist training carried on. Companies fired on the range at LA PANNERIE. Full marching order was worn so as to combine route marching with musketry training. Seven new officers arrived and were posted to the following companies	M.K.

Army Form C. 2118.

WAR DIARY
or
INTELLIGENCE SUMMARY.
(Erase heading not required.)

Instructions regarding War Diaries and Intelligence Summaries are contained in F. S. Regs., Part II. and the Staff Manual respectively. Title pages will be prepared in manuscript.

Place	Date	Hour	Summary of Events and Information	Remarks and references to Appendices
LE TOURET	19.7.16		Lieut. Cheape to D Coy. Lieut. Thomas S.E.B. to D Coy. 2nd Lt. Tierney to A Coy. 2nd Lt. Hennings to A Coy. 2nd Lt. Hill to B Coy. 2nd Lt. Machin to B Coy. 2nd Lt. Wilson to C Coy.	
	20.7.16		The 12th & 13th Batt'ns Royal Sussex relieved the 16th Sherwood Foresters in the	
FERME DU BOIS			right sub-section forming a composite battalion under the command of Lt. Col. Draffen. C&D Coys (18E) under the command of Capt'n Mayo (No 1 Coy) took over the right company frontage in the front line. A & B Coys under Lt. Ellis (No 2 Coy) [N°2 Coy] took over the right support company frontage. A&C Coys (13B) under the command of Capt'n Cassy took over the left coy. frontage front line. B&D Coys (13B) under Capt'n Tuthill took over the left support coy. frontage. The relief was carried out without a hitch and all companies reported complete by 11.34 p.m.	H.H.
FERME DU BOIS.	21.7.16		Intelligence. Rifle and machine gun fire carried on by both sides during the night weather fine and calm wind S.E. Two Boche aeroplanes crossed our lines about 8.a.m. but were driven back by fire from our anti-aircraft guns.	K.K.
	22.7.16		Enemy shelled support line lightly about 12.30 p.m chaperising a working party at about 1.a.m. this morning he shelled our front line parapet @ BOURNVILLE at the same time bombing his own wire. The Enemy appears to be thoroughly	

T.134. Wt. W708—776. 500000. 4/15. Sir J.C. & S.

Army Form C. 2118.

WAR DIARY
or
INTELLIGENCE SUMMARY.
(Erase heading not required.)

Instructions regarding War Diaries and Intelligence Summaries are contained in F. S. Regs., Part II. and the Staff Manual respectively. Title pages will be prepared in manuscript.

Place	Date	Hour	Summary of Events and Information	Remarks and references to Appendices
	22.7.16		disguised by our offensive operations and was constantly on the alert during the night a considerable amount of grass was cut by both companies. No hostile aeroplanes were seen.	
			Two new Officers joined the Battalion and were posted to the following companies 2nd Lt C Bartlett to C. Coy. 2nd Lt R.W Evans to A Coy.	MM
			During the night of the 22/23rd we carried out a minor gun operation against the enemy's parapet the Artillery co-operating. Enemy retaliation very feeble. The loss of 2nd Lt Easter (killed) was very much regretted.	MM
	23.7.16		Morning very quiet. we continued to harass the enemy with rifle grenades and fixed rifles, our snipers claimed several successes.	
			In the afternoon the enemy carried out a small bombardment of our front trench, presumably in retaliation for our Stokes' gun activity.	
			Battalion was relieved in the left sub sector by the 13th East Yorkshire Regt and moved to billets in the RUE L'EPINETTE. Hd qrs at S.19.b.1.5. B Coy in billets.	
	24.7.16		EPINETTE POST C Coy in CAILLOUX POSTS D Coy in billets. Relief asperted complete 6 pm.	
			The Battalion continued to share billets with the 12th Royal Sussex who occupied posts in FESTUBERT. Two next officers joined the battalion 2nd Lt Messies + 2nd Lt Gillan and were	

Army Form C. 2118.

WAR DIARY
or
INTELLIGENCE SUMMARY.
(Erase heading not required.)

Instructions regarding War Diaries and Intelligence Summaries are contained in F. S. Regs., Part II. and the Staff Manual respectively. Title pages will be prepared in manuscript.

Place	Date	Hour	Summary of Events and Information	Remarks and references to Appendices
RUE LEPINETTE	25.7.16		Posted to B and D Coys respectively. Companies bathed at the LE TOURET Baths. 3 Officers and 125 men were supplied for R.E. working parties.	
	26.7.16		do. do. Draft of 109 O.R. from the 4th & 5th Drafts carried to the Battalion and were posted as follows:— 25 to A Coy 24 to B Coy. 30 to C. Coy and 30 to D. Coy. A certain number had been in the D and A lines but the majority had not been out here before.	
	27.7.16		Draft talked at LE TOURET. The following Officers and O.R. went to MERVILLE to be invested by the G.O.C. 1st army. LT. E. ELLIS LT. CAPT WHITLEY Military Cross. (Nº 2896 Pte C. Davies Nº 3240 Pte R Smiley Nº 2641 A/Cpl G. Chambers Nº 2598 A/Sgt W.B. Mansell Nº 2854 Pte A Bailey Nº 2619 Pte d West Nº 5095 Pte F.A. Cooper Nº 3521 A/Cpl Bull Nº 2947 A/Cpl Knight.) Military Medal.	
FESTUBERT	28.7.16		The B.n relieved the 11th R. Sussex in the FESTUBERT LEFT Sub section and the following dispositions were assumed by the Coys. Right front company A Coy with one platoon of C in RICHMOND TERRACE. Left front company B Coy with one platoon of F coy in RICHMOND TERRACE. D Coy and the remaining two platoons of C Coy in the O.B.L.	

Army Form C. 2118.

WAR DIARY
or
INTELLIGENCE SUMMARY.
(Erase heading not required.)

Instructions regarding War Diaries and Intelligence Summaries are contained in F. S. Regs., Part II. and the Staff Manual respectively. Title pages will be prepared in manuscript.

Place	Date	Hour	Summary of Events and Information	Remarks and references to Appendices
FESTUBERT	28.7.16		Relief was reported complete by all companies	
	29.7.16		Day quiet on the whole intermittent hostile shelling of RICHMOND TERRACE. 4 Officers and 19 N.C.Os from the Westmorland and Cumberland Yeomanry attached to the Bn for instructional purposes. Night quiet our m.guns fired indirect on the Boche communications. In view of the possibility of a hostile raid on the battalion front strong defensive patrols were sent out accompanied by a machine gun.	
	30.7.16		Afternoon operations carried out by the Bn. according to the attached operation order. The operations were carried out both the execution of the smoke attack which was not possible owing to the direction and uncertainty of the wind. At about 2.15 a.m. a telephone message was received from the Brigade to the effect that the strong patrols could go out before the scheduled time The Lg Fusiliers The patrol was informed to that effect and the patrol anyway left owing to the mist and the extreme darkness of the night it was impossible to see more than a yard ahead and at about 3.5 a.m. loud talking was heard in the rear of Island 34 was being passed down to man the parapet and open rapid fire	

T.2134. Wt. W708—776. 500000. 4/15. Sir J. C. & S.

Army Form C. 2118.

WAR DIARY
or
INTELLIGENCE SUMMARY.
(Erase heading not required.)

Instructions regarding War Diaries and Intelligence Summaries are contained in F. S. Regs., Part II. and the Staff Manual respectively. Title pages will be prepared in manuscript.

Place	Date	Hour	Summary of Events and Information	Remarks and references to Appendices
FESTUBERT	30.7.16	3.5 a.m.	The patrol was ordered to stand fast, while enquiries were made as to its situation on the night. Owing to the darkness until 17th some time to head to find out where the garrison reported that a party of men had been seen in front of our wire. A voice was heard to say "come on boys. Lets get at them" followed by a shower of bombs which hit the feet of the parapet. Bombs were thrown back and fire opened with rifles and Lewis guns. Firing then ceased and it was found that the patrol for safe at 5.28.a.7.3½ had gone out about 2.45 a.m. but had not returned. Shortly afterwards some sentries of the patrol did return, and from questioning them it appeared that the patrol went out from about 23 led by 2nd Lt Macnaughton. They wandered about in the mist until they came to what they thought was the German Trench. They threw bombs and were promptly fired on by M. guns. They took cover in shell hole and after wandering about for some time then returned to our Trench. The only conclusion to be arrived at was that the patrol mistook by ideas for the enemy trench and not being able to find a way through the wire bombed the trench and was promptly fired on. They unfortunately suffered casualties and the loss of 2nd Lt Macnaughton killed and 8 ranks missing have to be reported.	

T-134. Wt. W708—776. 500000. 4/15. Sir J. C. & S.

Operation Order No 35   SECRET

1. (a). A raid will be carried out tonight in the enemy trenches between A.30.d.7½ and A.3.d.5½.5½ by the 14th Hants Regiment.
   (b) A feint attack will be made by the troops named in the margin between S.22.c.8.3½ and S.28.a.7.3½.

Lt Col. DRAFFEN.
13th R Sussex R.
116th L.T.M. Batt.
116th M.G. Co.
Rifle Grenade
Batteries under
Lt GAMMON.

2. The feint attack will be carried out as follows:—
   At 10 minutes before ZERO until 15 minutes after ZERO.

   (a) Smoke will be discharged from our trenches at selected points between QUINQUE CROSSING and CANADIAN ORCHARD, provided that the wind is favourable.

13th R Sussex R.
   The O.C. "D" Co will carry out this operation. 1500 bombs will be issued to him for this purpose.

   (b). At the same hour until ZERO 2 batteries R.F.A. will fire on the enemy parapet between S.28.a.7.3½ and S.22.c.8.5½.

R.F.A.
   At ZERO and until ZERO 15 mins. these Batteries will lift and form a barrage in rear.

Capt Finlay
116th L.T.M. Batt.
   (c). At 10 mins before ZERO until 15 mins after ZERO.
   A flank barrage will be formed against enemy trench from S.28.a.4.1 to S.28.a.7.3½ and from S.22.c.8.3½ to S.22.c.5½.6. (100 rounds per mortar will be fired).

Capt Finlay
3.7 Trench
Mortars
   (d) At the same time and for the same period, four 3.7 Trench mortars will be employed to fire smoke bombs and assist in forming a smoke screen.

2nd Lt GAMMON.
Rifle grenade
Batteries.
   (e) At 10 minutes before ZERO until 15 minutes after ZERO.
   Rifle grenade batteries will assist in forming the flank barrage from S.28.a.4.1 to S.28.a.7.3½ and from S.22.c.8.3½ to S.22.c.5½.6. 10 rifle grenade batteries will be employed on each flank.

116th M.G.Co.
   (f) At 10 minutes before ZERO until 2 hours after ZERO, the 116th M.G.Co will fire indirect on EITEL ALLEY NORTH, EITEL ALLEY SOUTH and ADALBERT ROAD.

13th R Sussex R.
No 1 Patrol.
Lt Thomas.
10 N.C.O's & men
D Co.
1 Lewis gun &
3 men.

No 2 Patrol
10 N.C.O's & men
of A Co.
1 Lewis gun &
3 men.

   (g) At 1½ hours after ZERO.
   Strong patrols as per margin will go out and endeavour to secure prisoners.
   They will make for the following gaps in enemy wire and enter his trench if opportunity offers.
   No 1 Patrol will make for gap in wire at S.22.c.8.3½.
   No 2 Patrol will make for gap in wire at S.28.a.7.3½.

3. ZERO hour will be 1.30am.
4. Countersign will be "WILTSHIRE"
5. Report to Hdqrs 1st Royal Sussex Regt. O.B.L.

   H. Cophead
   Capt & Adjt.

30.7.16

Copy No 1 to O.C. 13th R Sus R.
      2   O.C. 116th L.T.M. Batt.
      3   O.C. 116th M.G.Co.
      4   O.C. Rifle Grenade Batts.
    5, 6 & 7 O.C. A. B & D Coys.
      8   Hdqrs 116th Brigade
      9   Office Copy.

116th Brigade.
39th Division.
6-------------

13th BATTALION

THE ROYAL SUSSEX REGIMENT

AUGUST 1 9 1 6

Vol 6

D.6

Confidential

War Diary
of
13 Bn. R. Sussex R.

From 1st August 1916 to 31 August 1916

Army Form C. 2118.

WAR DIARY
or
INTELLIGENCE SUMMARY.
(Erase heading not required.)

Instructions regarding War Diaries and Intelligence Summaries are contained in F. S. Regs., Part II. and the Staff Manual respectively. Title pages will be prepared in manuscript.

Place	Date	Hour	Summary of Events and Information	Remarks and references to Appendices
FESTUBERT	1.8.16		Day quiet on the whole. Intermittent shelling of the front line with whizz-bangs. In the afternoon at about 4.30 pm the enemy registered on ROPE STREET with 5.9" howitzers doing slight damage. The Battalion was relieved by the 1/1st Herts regiment. Specialists were relieved by daylight. Guides met the incoming companies at the junction of RUE L'EPINETTE and RUE DU BOIS 9.45 pm. All companies reported relief complete 11.50 pm. Companies marched independently to billets about ESSARS all in billets reported 3.3 am.	
ESSARS	2.8.16		Training spent in interior economy, kit inspections etc. Afternoon devoted to bathing. 2nd Lt CA= Whitley left to join the Royal Flying Corps.	
	3.8.16		Training of bombers, snipers, Lewis gunners, scouts with gunners, carried on. Band reorganised under Cpl Smith. Battalion route march 4.15 pm — 8 pm.	
	4.8.16		Training of bombers, snipers etc carried on. Battalion route march took place 2nd Anniversary of the declaration of war shot services held.	
	5.8.16		Training programme continued.	
	6.8.16		Special parade service held in BETHUNE at which the Army Commander was present	

Army Form C. 2118.

WAR DIARY
or
INTELLIGENCE SUMMARY.
(Erase heading not required.)

Instructions regarding War Diaries and Intelligence Summaries are contained in F. S. Regs., Part II. and the Staff Manual respectively. Title pages will be prepared in manuscript.

Place	Date	Hour	Summary of Events and Information	Remarks and references to Appendices
ESSARS	6.8.16	cont?	Battalion relieved the 17th King's Royal Rifles in Brigade Reserve GIVENCHY SECTION and took over Billets about GORRE. Companies marched independently to Billets — all in Billets reported 8.17 p.m.	
GORRE	7.8.16		Training of Bombers, Lewis gunners ad instruction in wiring carried on — Baths allotted to the Battalion — working parties also found. Extract from London Gazette … Right Reg. Major J. Shanne to be Temp. Quartermaster and Hon. Lieut … 21st July 1916. Bethune shelled.	
	8.8.16		Large working parties found — Training of Bombers & Lewis gunners continued when not Brigade working parties. Bombs dropped on Bethune from hostile aircraft early in the morning.	
	9.8.16		Large working parties found and Training of Bombers — Snipers and Lewis gunners continued.	
	10.8.16		Baths allotted to the Battalion — working parties found and MARAIS POSTS Thoroughly cleaned up and put in a proper state of repair... C.S.M. Clarke J.A. appointed acting Regt. Seg. Major Vice S. Major T. Shanne promoted dated 6.8.16.	
	11.8.16		Batts. allotted to the Battalion. The Battalion were relieved by the 19th Manchester Regiment (21st Brigade) the morning commencing at 8.40 p.m. All Companies reported relief (with G.G.) at 9.35 p.m. Companies marched off via NORTH BANK of CANAL (La Bassée) to Bethune (with its Transport) concentrating at the N.W. end of the Town at the junction of the Bethune — Choquen Road and Bethune—Hinges Roads. The Battalion then marched Via main BETHUNE – CHOQUES ROAD through the latter Town to LE BOUDON when Tea (carried in the cookers) was provided afterwards proceeding to billets about LOZINGHEM. All in Billets reported at 4.30 am 12.8.16. Capt. & H. Bowley Temporary attached	

T.1134. Wt. W708–776. 500000. 4/15. Sir J. C. & S.

Army Form C. 2118.

WAR DIARY
or
INTELLIGENCE SUMMARY.
(Erase heading not required.)

Instructions regarding War Diaries and Intelligence Summaries are contained in F. S. Regs., Part II. and the Staff Manual respectively. Title pages will be prepared in manuscript.

Place	Date	Hour	Summary of Events and Information	Remarks and references to Appendices
LOZINGHEM	12.8.16		to the Battalion	
			Battalion reveille – Kit inspection – cleaning equipment and polishing of all buttons and fittings on tunics	
	13.8.16		Battalion marched from LOZINGHEM at 5.40 a.m. marching via AUCHEL, PERNES, OURTON to the South side of the BOIS DU HAZOIS where it bivouacked for the day remaining there from 10 a.m. to 5.30 p.m. Proceeding at 5.30 p.m. the Battalion marched via LA COMTÉ, LE PETIT RIETZ and HOUVELIN to billets about MAGNICOURT EN COMTÉ within the MONCHY BRETON Training Area of the 3rd Army to which the Brigade is being attached. All in billets (with the exception of officers for whom it was exceptionally difficult to obtain suitable billets) was reported at 8.35 p.m. Cocoa made in the Cookers was provided on the road at 6.40 p.m.	
MAGNICOURT EN	14.8.16		Brigade (Battalion) attached to 17th Corps, 3rd Army for Training. Whole day spent in Training grounds.	
-COMTÉ	15.8.16		Training in MONCHY BRETON TRAINING AREA	
	to			
	22.8.16			
MONCHEAUX	23.8.16		The 39th Division moved to the MARIEUX area – the Battalion marched to billets in MONCHEAUX (about 11 miles) and staged the night	
IVERGNY	24.8.16		Battalion marched to billets in IVERGNY (about 4 miles) and rested till 8 am 25.8.16.	

Army Form C. 2118.

WAR DIARY
or
INTELLIGENCE SUMMARY.
(Erase heading not required.)

Place	Date	Hour	Summary of Events and Information	Remarks and references to Appendices
BOIS DU WARNIMONT	25.8.16		BATTALION continued to march EN ROUTE to WARNIMONT Wood and came under the orders of the Reserve Army. Route LUCHEUX - HALLOY - THIEVRES. Battalion arrived at 3.20 p.m. and bivouaced in wood. The 39 Division came under the orders of the Reserve Army from midnight August 24/25.	
	26.8.16		Battalion rested. 2/Lieut B. WHEATLEY joined for duty and was taken on the strength. Improvement and cleaning up of cantonments.	
	27.8.16		Church of England Service at 11.30 a.m. 39 Division continued move in relief of 6 Division and Battalion marched to WOOD near MAILLY.	
WOOD (B.17) NEAR MAILLY	28.8.16		MAILLY where bivouaced. Temp. Lts ELLIS, ELPHICKE and FABIAN posted. Temp: Report on whilst in Brevan? of Companies.	
MAILLY	29.8.16		Officers and N.C.O.'s and Runners reconnoitred line NORTH of River ANCRE. BATTALION to be in Support to 11 Batt. and 14 Brig.	
	30.8.16		Wet day and battalion worked through by enemy. Reconnoitring continued. Shells fell close to C. Company's quarters doing no hurt.	
	31.8.16		Shells again fell near Battalion and Trenches dug for protection.	

J.B. Brafferton Lt Col
Commdg 13th Royal Fusiliers

116th Brigade
39th Division.

13th BATTALION

THE ROYAL SUSSEX REGIMENT

SEPTEMBER 1916

Headquarters 116th Infantry Brigade

Herewith War Diary for September.
Kindly acknowledge receipt

Onward 2/Lt
a/Adjt
for Lieut Col
1-10-16.   Commanding 13 Royal Sussex Regt.

Q/8/12.

Army Form C. 2118.

WAR DIARY
or
INTELLIGENCE SUMMARY.

(Erase heading not required.)

Instructions regarding War Diaries and Intelligence Summaries are contained in F. S. Regs., Part II. and the Staff Manual respectively. Title pages will be prepared in manuscript.

Place	Date	Hour	Summary of Events and Information	Remarks and references to Appendices
WOOD (p17) NEAR MAILLY	1·9·16		Officers, N.C.Os and Runners reconnoitred the line N. of river ANCRE and E. of HAMEL. Draft of 25 other ranks reported and were taken on the strength. The Battalion moved into the line and took up it's assembly positions for the attack to be made the next day.	Miss Brown (E)
MAILLET	2·9·16		Report on Operations.	
HAMEL	3·9·16		1. On the night of 2/3rd The Battalion took up it's assembly positions in trenches and dug outs in HAMEL. The movement was completed by about 11 p.m. All men were given hot coffee and rum in the early morning of the 3rd.	
			2. At zero hour (5·10 a.m.) as the assaulting troops left their positions of Assembly C, D Companies under Capt ELPHICKE and 2nd Lieut STORY, which were (10th off) in Support 11th Batt. ROYAL SUSSEX REGT, moved into the following positions of readiness - C. Company E. of PECHE STREET in the Old British front line, D. Company W. of PECHE STREET in the Old British front line. A Company under Capt FABIAN (having one Platoon shot got cut off) moved into GORDON TRENCH and B Company under 2nd Lieut HOPWOOD moved into ROBERTS TRENCH one Platoon going into LOUVERCY STREET.	D·7
			3. At about 5·25 a.m. C. Company left the Old British line E. of PECHE STREET and moved forward into No MAN'S LAND taking cover behind a RIDGE N.E. of PECHE STREET	

Army Form C. 2118.

WAR DIARY
or
INTELLIGENCE SUMMARY.
(Erase heading not required.)

Instructions regarding War Diaries and Intelligence Summaries are contained in F.S. Regs., Part II. and the Staff Manual respectively. Title pages will be prepared in manuscript.

Place	Date	Hour	Summary of Events and Information	Remarks and references to Appendices
HAMEL	3.9.16		When the movements were completed D. Company moved from W of PECHE STREET into PECHE STREET – by this time all the Officers of C. Company had become casualties and 2/Lieut STORY took Command of both C & D Companies (being 2/Lieut HENNING in Command of C. Company 2/Lieut HENNING got in touch with the reserve company of the 11th Batt. ROYAL SUSSEX REGT whose Commander informed him that he had received further orders not to move until he received further orders from his CO. After waiting for some time 2/Lt Storey ordered C. Company to move forward to support the other Companies of the 11th Batt. This Company advanced on the ridge to be met by a heavy burst of machine gun fire – 2/Lieut Henning and several men were wounded, the remainder falling back behind the ridge. 2/LIEUT STOREY then took forward D Company part of B Company and a few men of the RIFLE BRIGADE (Stragglers). Unfortunately direction was lost and the party instead of bearing to the RIGHT to support the 11th Batt. swung round too much to the LEFT and entered the Enemy Trenches which were totally knocked about by shell fire. 2/Lt STOREY stayed in this trench for about two hours without being attacked but being heavily shelled during the whole time. He pushed out Patrols to his right & left but did not get into touch with any of our own Troops. One of the Patrols reported that our Troops were withdrawing to our own trenches so ultimately 2/Lt STOREY withdrew his men to the RIDGE in NOMAN'S LAND in	

Army Form C. 2118.

WAR DIARY
or
INTELLIGENCE SUMMARY.
(Erase heading not required.)

Place	Date	Hour	Summary of Events and Information	Remarks and references to Appendices
HAMEL	3.9.16		which the 11th Batt. had advanced. 2nd Lt STOREY then re-organized his party and went to LANCASHIRE POST where he got into communication with his Commanding Officer at KENTISH CAVE. It was informed that the 11th Batt. were still in the enemy's line and ordered to at once advance to their support but before he could do this further orders were received that no further advance was to take place. On the left, A Company commanded [blank] with GORDON TRENCH as the assaulting troops went forward — before the whole Company could enter shouts were heard of "Retire, Retire" and a Sergeant with 9 men from the assaulting Columns principally 11th Brigade came hurrying back over the top into the Trench making movement almost impossible — Capt FABIAN attempted to rally his men and started "C" Coy on A Company [B.?] — As many men as could retire came towards the enemy's lines — about 70 yards away from the enemy this gallant Officer had two fingers blown off his right hand but he continued to press on until this time was killed. Soon after the survivors took cover in shell holes and ultimately crawled back to our lines. The advance commenced a very heavy artillery barrage was opened on GORDON TRENCH and ROBERTS TRENCH. S.B. Company which took field with ROBERTS TRENCH at the commencement of the advance then went forward to GORDON TRENCH and 2nd Lt HOPWOOD took forward to the German lines as heavy	

Army Form C. 2118.

Instructions regarding War Diaries and Intelligence Summaries are contained in F. S. Regs., Part II. and the Staff Manual respectively. Title pages will be prepared in manuscript.

WAR DIARY
or
INTELLIGENCE SUMMARY.
(Erase heading not required.)

Place	Date	Hour	Summary of Events and Information	Remarks and references to Appendices
HAMEL	3.9.16		him as he could collect & but nothing more was seen of these officers. An intense bombardment of the Trenches continued for several hours causing many casualties and owing to the breaking of units and congestion in the Trenches all attempts at re-organisation failed. b. K. Ennis 1st Battalion were withdrawn to Prime Ext.- Our casualties were:- **Officers** Capt. FABIAN ⎫ Lieut. Cheaps ⎬ Killed 2Lieut Ormsby ⎭ Capt. Elphicke ⎫ 2Lieut Henning ⎪ 2Lieut Wilson ⎬ Wounded 2Lieut Mackin ⎭ Lieut. Thomas ⎫ missing 2Lieut Hopwood ⎬ 2Lieut Barrow ⎭ Lieut Dunning R.A.M.C. and 2Lieut BARTLETT wounded at Duty **Other Ranks** Killed — Died of Wounds — Missing — Wounded — Wounded at Duty 8 — 3 — 26 — 71 — 15	

Army Form C. 2118.

WAR DIARY
or
INTELLIGENCE SUMMARY.
(Erase heading not required.)

Instructions regarding War Diaries and Intelligence Summaries are contained in F. S. Regs., Part II. and the Staff Manual respectively. Title pages will be prepared in manuscript.

Place	Date	Hour	Summary of Events and Information	Remarks and references to Appendices
HAMEL	3.9.16		Total casualties all ranks 135.	
			Lieut Cheape (Field Works Officer) was ordered to take over A Company which lost its officers. This work throughout the operation was exceedingly valuable, and it was only after he had completed it and was attending to wounded men that he was killed. It was helping to carry a wounded man away on a stretcher when he was obstinately sniped and died within a very few minutes. A draft of 112 other ranks reported for duty and was taken on the strength.	
PROWIE FORT	4.9.16		The Battalion was heavily shelled in the afternoon and lost two signallers killed. At 6 p.m. relief was received & returned to the bivouacs in WOOD P.17 W. of MAILLY-MAILLET. A wet night.	
WOOD P.17	5.9.16		Draft of 70 other ranks reported for duty and were taken on the strength. – Working parties to collect tools and clear up trenches at HAMEL were provided.	
	6.9.16		Working parties provided to dig trench for signals. – Battalion moved to huts in BERTRANCOURT.	
BERTRANCOURT	7.9.16		Company drill, bayonet fighting, musketry and Bombing, machine gunners & signallers training under their respective officers. General cleaning and clearing up of Camps. Draft of 70 other ranks reported for duty and were taken on the strength.	
	8.9.16		Officers NCOs Runners reconnoitred left sub sector BEAUMONT HAMEL. 5·9" shells dropped near the Camp during the day. No damage or hurt.	

Army Form C. 2118.

WAR DIARY
or
INTELLIGENCE SUMMARY.
(Erase heading not required.)

Place	Date	Hour	Summary of Events and Information	Remarks and references to Appendices
BERTRAN COURT	9.9.16		Line reconnoitred by Officers, NCO's & Runners. – Divisional band attended camps at 5 p.m. Working party provided for fatigue	
BEAUMONT HAMEL SECTOR	10.9.16		Relieved 1/5 Gloucestershire Regt in left Subsector of BEAUMONT HAMEL. Relief complete 1.30 p.m. A and B Companies in front line – C Company (WHITE CITY) and D Company in Reserve (the BOWERY) a great deal of drainage and general Trench maintenance and clearing up work done – Ambulance put out in front of CLIVE STREET – a Patrol went out to examine wire and graves – graves quite short	
	11.9.16		Gap cut in Enemy wire at Q5 a 3. 3.3/4. and kept open at night by our Lewis Guns. – Communication Trenches 4" AVENUE and 5" AVENUE improved and cleaned and a great deal of work down in front line Trenches in making fire steps and improving generally – Wire put out in front of CLIVE TRENCH and our extemporised wire reconstructed and improved – Snipers posts constructed and Machine Gun Emplacement in 4" AVENUE converted into an O.P. Patrols report Enemy wire exceedingly strong	
	12.9.16		General Trench maintenance and improvement of Trenches and Latrines, a lot of work done – New Latrines constructed in HUNTERS STREET and BOWERY. Wire put out in front of CLIVE STREET, NORTH STREET and HUNTER STREET. – HUNTER STREET deepened and Trench connecting right front Company with next Battalion commenced. Medium Trench Mortar attempted to cut away a new	
	13.9.16		at Q5 a 1. 1/2. but owing to a premature explosion failed to complete its work. Wire put out in front of CLIVE STREET and HUNTER STREET. New Trench connecting with Battalion on	

Army Form C. 2118.

WAR DIARY
or
INTELLIGENCE SUMMARY.
(Erase heading not required.)

Instructions regarding War Diaries and Intelligence Summaries are contained in F.S. Regs., Part II. and the Staff Manual respectively. Title pages will be prepared in manuscript.

Place	Date	Hour	Summary of Events and Information	Remarks and references to Appendices
BEAUMONT HAMEL SECTOR.	13.9.16		Night completed. Draft of 79 other ranks reported for duty and were taken on the strength.	
	14.9.16		Relieved by 1/4 Hampshire Regt. Relief complete at 1 p.m. and all in Billets at MAILLY-MAILLET at 3.30 p.m. Battalion in Brigade Support. During the 4 days in the Trenches the enemy were fairly active but our artillery was considerably more active and showed a very definite superiority over that of the enemy. Battalion attacked Serre - a draft of 31 other ranks reported for duty and were taken on the strength	
MAILLY-MAILLET	15.9.16		Working parties provided for drawing and truck boarding Communication Trenches - for carrying of gas cylinders to front line and loading and unloading R.E. materials - Remainder of Battalion attended training. Fighting Patrols under 2/Lt C BARTLETT and 2nd Lt F.E. TIERNEY failed to find gap in enemy's wire and returned after finding enemy very much on the alert. No casualty (1 wounded)	
	16.9.16		Working parties provided as on previous day - MAILLY MAILLET shelled at 9 p.m. and again later rather heavier - no casualties	
	17.9.16		Working parties as for 15th - Village again shelled at 8.15 p.m. a draft of 2 men reported for duty and were taken on the strength	
	18.9.16		Officers NCOs and Runners reconnoitred the right Battalion frontage REDAN SECTION preparatory to the Battalion taking over that part of the line from the 25th ROYAL FUSILIERS - 2nd Lieut G.A. WELLS reported for duty and was taken on the strength and posted G.B. Company	
REDAN RIDGE	19.9.16		REDAN RIDGE right Battalion frontage taken over from 25th ROYAL FUSILIERS - Relief completed 1.30 p.m.	

Army Form C. 2118.

WAR DIARY
or
INTELLIGENCE SUMMARY.
(Erase heading not required.)

Instructions regarding War Diaries and Intelligence Summaries are contained in F. S. Regs., Part II. and the Staff Manual respectively. Title pages will be prepared in manuscript.

Place	Date	Hour	Summary of Events and Information	Remarks and references to Appendices
REDAN RIDGE	19.9.16		An officer's Patrol under 2nd Lt F.E. TIERNEY went out to examine Enemy's wire in which it was alleged there was a gap, but they came across a strong fighting Patrol of the Enemy and withdrew. In the evening but caused immediately our artillery opened. 2nd LIEUT A.H. STORY promoted Temp Captain whilst in Command of a Company. A draft of 201 other ranks reported for duty and arms taken on their strength. This draft consisted of at the Transport lines BERTRANCOURT under Brigade orders. Enemy shelled our support line - 5.9 shells falling	
	20.9.16		near CHATHAM TRENCH, FREDDY STREET and BURROW TRENCH all of which were damaged. Our field guns and 4.2 Howitzers shelled the Enemy's Trenches during the afternoon and evening. 2nd Lieuts B.C. COULDREY and H.B. LANGDALE reports for duty and were taken on the Strength and posted to D Company. A quieter day - a great deal of work done in repairing, preventing Trenches also cleaning and	
	21.9.6		checkerboarding them - the reflection in the sky of a big fire in the direction of THIEPVAL was at about 10 p.m. and lasted for over an hour. Patrols this area shell holes in NO MAN'S LAND our wire and enemy's wire particularly strong and made no attempt to cross -	
	22.9.6		Draft of 201 moved to MAILLY-MAILLET and were detailed for working parties. CHATHAM and b. AVENUE were damaged by Enemy's Heavy Trench Mortars in the early afternoon this in retaliation for our medium Trench mortars cutting Enemy's wire earlier in the day.	
	23.9.6		Draft joined the Battalion. Artillery on both sides active - a great deal of work done in repairing improved Trenches, digging outs and Latrines - a great deal of S.A.A. and bombs salved. An enemy howitzer fell in CHATHAM TRENCH at 2.30 pm killing 9 other ranks & of those had only returned in the earlier in the day.	

T2134. Wt. W708—776. 500000. 4/15. Sir J. C. & S.

Army Form C. 2118.

WAR DIARY
or
INTELLIGENCE SUMMARY.
(Erase heading not required.)

Instructions regarding War Diaries and Intelligence Summaries are contained in F. S. Regs., Part II. and the Staff Manual respectively. Title pages will be prepared in manuscript.

Place	Date	Hour	Summary of Events and Information	Remarks and references to Appendices
REDAN RIDGE	24.9.16		Enemy fired Heavy Trench mortars on CHATHAM and FREDDY STREET in the afternoon Cutting the Telephone wires in three separate occasions. In the evening Lachrymatory shells fell near the support line. Our artillery was active throughout the day and our Medium Trench mortars continued cutting enemy wire at 6 p.m. Working parties are on the previous days.	
	25.9.16		Enemy particularly quiet and supine apparent a party of his working behind his 2nd line. Our artillery was immediately informed and opening quickly we obtained success. A quantity of work done in cutting enemy Trenches etc. as on previous days. A premature from one of our Trench guns fell in WHITE CITY. Details for a demonstration on our front received. If reinforcements were brought to the left of H and dummy figures to be hoisted in 15 sec parapet with a view to deceiving the Enemy and drawing his fire out in anticipation of large operations taking place in the day to the south. At zero 12.15 p.m. rapid independent — Our artillery heavily bombarded the enemy's Trenches throughout the afternoon & night until the night drawing off, replied however. The enemy accepted our front their parapet with machine gun fire for about half an hour beginning shortly after our artillery opened up. Very fine shells of large caliber were fired by the Enemy throughout the afternoon but his heavy Trench mortars were very active also ranged at 33 throughs were sent over in retaliation.	
	26.9.16		Very little activity on the part of the Enemy. A shot from one of our Trench guns exploded in the front line. (A(4))	
	27.9.16		No one was hurt but the Trench considerably damaged. 2nd LIEUTS F.H. LAKE and H.C. KEOGH reported	

T2134. Wt. W708–776. 500060. 4/15. Sir J. C. & 8.

Army Form C. 2118.

WAR DIARY
or
INTELLIGENCE SUMMARY.
(Erase heading not required.)

Instructions regarding War Diaries and Intelligence Summaries are contained in F.S. Regs., Part II. and the Staff Manual respectively. Title pages will be prepared in manuscript.

Place	Date	Hour	Summary of Events and Information	Remarks and references to Appendices
REDAN RIDGE	27.9.16		On duty and were taken on the strength and posted to A and B Companies respectively - 2' Lieut MASTERS. Transferred to England sick and struck off the strength.	
	28.9.16		Enemy much more active than on previous day - Gas shells fired at our batteries to the rear of WHITE CITY in the evening. Our artillery opened heavy bombardment on our right in the direction of THIEPVAL at 1 pm and a regular and continuous bombardment followed for the rest of the day and night on into the night. Batteries to our rear fired across and gas shells were fired at enemy batteries throughout the afternoon and evening. Our Trenches were somewhat damaged by heavy Trench mortars and 5.9 shells between 1.30 and 3 pm.	
	29.9.16		Enemy's artillery more active and 5.9 shells fell near CHATHAM TRENCH and BUSTER STREET also near JUNCTION of MOUNT JOY and ROMAN ROAD damaging Trenches near our Tanks. A great deal of work was done in repairing and improving the Trenches also enlarging and strengthening dug outs and chief-bombing Communication Trenches. A Patrol found enemy's wire rather extensive, thick and strong.	
	30.9.16		Enemy's artillery fired a few 5.9 and H.S. Shrapnel at batteries behind our front and the cut our a large number of Rifle Grenades on the front Trenches of the Left Front Company - Our howitzers by arrangement did not bombard. Later about 150 yards from junction of SIXTH AVENUE with front line - the front line being partially well drawn for this purpose. 22 shells were fired 15 of which failed to explode but damage was done, work was continued as on previous days. Patrol failed to find.	

T2134. Wt. W708—776. 500060. 4/15. Sir J. C. & S.

Army Form C. 2118.

WAR DIARY
or
INTELLIGENCE SUMMARY.
(Erase heading not required.)

Instructions regarding War Diaries and Intelligence Summaries are contained in F. S. Regs., Part II. and the Staff Manual respectively. Title pages will be prepared in manuscript.

Place	Date	Hour	Summary of Events and Information	Remarks and references to Appendices
REDAN RIDGE	30.9.16		Any gaps in the enemy wire which were exceptionally wide and strong — none of the enemy were encountered — No enemy aeroplanes were seen but our own were very active and drew enemy machine gun fire as well as shrapnel.	
	1st October 1916.			

G.W. Daffern, Lieut Col.
Commanding 13th Royal Sussex Regt.

T2134. Wt. W708—776. 500000. 4/15. Sir J. C. & S.

116th Brigade.
39th Division.

13th BATTALION

THE ROYAL SUSSEX REGIMENT

OCTOBER 1916

Confidential

War Diary
of
13th Bn. Royal Sussex R.
for the month of
Oct 1916

Army Form C. 2118.

WAR DIARY
or
INTELLIGENCE SUMMARY.
(Erase heading not required.)

Place	Date	Hour	Summary of Events and Information	Remarks and references to Appendices
REDAN RIDGE	1.10.16		Enemy's artillery was mostly quiet. His trench mortars were active especially at night, also several Rifle Grenades fell near 6th AVENUE. His machine gun's fixed vindict on to SUNKEN ROAD and just behind WHITE CITY. Our artillery was active and dispersed working parties observed by our snipers 5 to 6 S.E. of SERRE. A great deal of work was done in repairing, clearing and deckboarding Trenches. Also constructing and enlarging dug outs (i.e. superior). SAA and bombs ration and cleaned. A patrol reconnoitred crater 150 yards E. of junction of 6th AVENUE with FRONT LINE also disused Trench running N. from Crater. Latter had the appearance of having been occasionally used but none of the enemy was encountered.	
	2.10.16 3.10.16		A quiet day. Work continued as on previous day. Raining in the morning and afternoon. Nothing of importance. Orders 5 Relief, 1/1 Herts Regt. in Y Ravine sector successive. Enemy's artillery more active and shells fell near WHITE CITY between 1 and 2:30 p.m. Also in neighbourhood of the BOWERY and battalions to the rear of our position. H.E. shrapnel used. Relieved by 23rd Batt. Royal Fusiliers at 4 p.m. and battalion proceeds via 4th AVENUE, AUCHONVILLERS and TIPPERARY AVENUE to Y RAVINE SECTOR in relief of 1/1 Batt. Herts Regt. — Relief complete 8 p.m. C. & D. Companies in front line — B Company in supports and A Company in Reserve. A quiet night.	
Y. RAVINE	4.10.16		In afternoon enemy shelled front line trench and wire entanglements — also shrapnel was burst between front and support lines. His artillery was active during the morning and shelled AUCHONVILLERS at 8:30 p.m. B Company took over right Company's frontage of 1st 11th Batt Royal Sussex and A Company extended its left	

Army Form C. 2118.

WAR DIARY
or
INTELLIGENCE SUMMARY.
(Erase heading not required.)

Instructions regarding War Diaries and Intelligence Summaries are contained in F. S. Regs, Part II. and the Staff Manual respectively. Title pages will be prepared in manuscript.

Place	Date	Hour	Summary of Events and Information	Remarks and references to Appendices
Y. RAVINE	4/10/16		Of RESERVE LINE Covering front taken over. Relief completed 7 p.m. - D. & A. Coys in the right front, C. Company in the Centre (front) B. Company on the LEFT front and A. Company in RESERVE LINE covering the 3 other Companies.	
	5.10.16		Considerable shelling of front line and Support Trenches by enemy artillery but on the whole other Battalion's Casualties were slight. Our Medium Trench Mortars bombarded the enemy's 'wire' and	
	9.10.16		front trenches successfully, his retaliation was fairly heavy and the considerable damage to our Trenches. On the 8th inst. Capt J.A. ROBINSON, Lieut. H. FOX and 2Lieut. R.G. CHALLIS reported for duty. was from the Depth.	
ENGLEBELMER	10.10.16		The Battalion was relieved in the Y RAVINE Sector by the 14th BATT. HANTS REGT - and moved to	
WOOD			bivouacs in ENGLEBELMER WOOD - All in camp at 3/5 a.m. R. Coy billeted in AUCHONVILLERS	
	11.10.16		Baths started and proved a great success. Company Platoon drills and all Ranks completed with equipment etc. Baths at MAILLY MAILLET allotted to Battalion	
	12.10.16		Company and Platoon drill - Working parties furnished	
REDAN SECTION	13.10.16		The Battalion relieved the 12 BATT ROYAL SUSSEX REGT in the RIGHT REDAN SECTOR - Relief complete at 1.30 p.m. A. Coy took over Right front Coys frontage - B. Coy took over Left front Coys frontage - D Coy took over Left front Coys frontage and C. Coy were in RESERVE in the BOWERY	
	14.10.16		Except for shelling intermittently the enemy was mostly inactive	

T2134. Wt. W708—776. 500000. 4/15. Sir J. C. & S.

Army Form C. 2118.

WAR DIARY
or
INTELLIGENCE SUMMARY.
(Erase heading not required.)

Instructions regarding War Diaries and Intelligence Summaries are contained in F. S. Regs., Part II. and the Staff Manual respectively. Title pages will be prepared in manuscript.

Place	Date	Hour	Summary of Events and Information	Remarks and references to Appendices
REDAN SECTION	15.10.16		Enemy shelled WHITE CITY and communication trenches intermittently. Not on the whole a quiet day.	
REDOUBT RIGHT SECTION	16.10.16		The Battalion was relieved by the NELSON BATTALION ROYAL NAVAL DIVISION and proceeded GENGELBELMER WOOD where after resting for the holiday meal the Battalion moved on through AVELUY and WOOD POST to the REDOUBT SECTION in relief of the 8th SOUTH LANCASHIRE REGT — Relief complete 3:30 am on the 17th inst. A Company in BAINBRIDGE TRENCH — HEADQUARTERS in ZOLLERN TRENCH — B and D Companies in SCHWABEN TRENCH and C Company in BUGAR TRENCH	
	17.10.16 to 19.10.16		Preparations for attack to be made up on STUFF TRENCH, digging French shallow up STUFF Communication Trench with BAINBRIDGE TRENCH also commencing Communication Trench from BAINBRIDGE TRENCH to TRENCH to be captured — learning dumps behind BAINBRIDGE TRENCH starting R.E. material.	
	20.10.16		The Battalion was relieved by the 11th BATT ROYAL SUSSEX Regt and spent the day and night of the 20/21st at WOOD POST.	
	21.10.16		The Battalion proceeded to the right sub section of the REDOUBT SECTION preparatory to the attack on STUFF TRENCH which was to be made in conjunction with the 11th Batt Royal Sussex Regt. — Deployment B and C Companies assaulting Companies — Two platoons of D Company in right kelp of BAINBRIDGE TRENCH — Two platoons of D Company and A Company in SCHWABEN TRENCH — BATT HEADQUARTERS (with 11th BATT HEADQUARTERS) in ZOLLERN TRENCH	

Army Form C. 2118.

WAR DIARY
or
INTELLIGENCE SUMMARY.
(Erase heading not required.)

Instructions regarding War Diaries and Intelligence Summaries are contained in F. S. Regs., Part II. and the Staff Manual respectively. Title pages will be prepared in manuscript.

Place	Date	Hour	Summary of Events and Information	Remarks and references to Appendices
REDOUBT SECTION	21.10.16		Report on Operations.	

At 11 am B and C Companies moved up from SCHWABEN TRENCH in artillery formation and on nearing BAINBRIDGE TRENCH extended in 3 separate lines on a frontage of approximately 250 yds B Company on the right with it's right flank resting on the Communication Trench leading from STUFF REDOUBT to STUFF TRENCH and C Company on the left in touch with the right flank of the 11th Batt Royal Inniskg Regt. These two Companies were in their assembly positions of three waves by 11.40 am. The first wave about 30 yds in front of BAINBRIDGE TRENCH the second wave immediately in front of that Trench and the third wave just behind that Trench. At 12.6 Noon the artillery commenced and our own afty fire by 2nd Lieut F.E.O. COUCHMAN (Commanding B Company) and 2nd Lieut H.S. LANGDALE (Commanding C Company) advanced very close up to our artillery barrage and entered STUFF TRENCH in perfect line. In the main not much opposition was encountered except on the right flank — A strong bombing party had been told off by B Company to deal with the Communication Trench on our right flank and here some opposition was met with but after some 40 minutes afterwards bombing this in the STUFF TRENCH and the Whole of STUFF TRENCH and Communication Trench 50 yds above the line of our own and the Whole of STUFF TRENCH were in our hands. For the rest of the day the captured position was heavily shelled but no counter-attack was launched by the enemy. It was very noticeable that the

T2134. Wt. W708-776. 500000. 4/15. Sir J. C. & S.

Army Form C. 2118.

WAR DIARY
or
INTELLIGENCE SUMMARY.
(Erase heading not required.)

Place	Date	Hour	Summary of Events and Information	Remarks and references to Appendices
STUFF TRENCH	21-10-16		Enemy artillery was concentrated on STUFF TRENCH and BAINBRIDGE TRENCH and he did not shell much further which. The work of consolidation was at once commenced and touch was gained with the Battalions on our right which had also advanced and taken the left portion of REGINA TRENCH. During the afternoon S.A.A. Bombs and water and sandbags were carried up to the captured position. The 11th Batt. Royal Irish Rifles on our left had suffered considerably more than our Batt. and when a Company of the 12th Batt. Royal Irish Rifles arrived at Martinsart by arrangement with the O.C. of the 11th Royal Irish Rifles, 2 platoons of the Company were sent into the left of STUFF TRENCH and the other Two Platoons into BAINBRIDGE TRENCH in support.	
	22-10-16		Except for intermittent shelling the night proved fairly quiet and shortly before dawn two Platoons of C Company were relieved by 2 Platoons of D Company and withdrawn to SCHWABEN TRENCH. It was also thought advisable 5 P.M. out our line and accordingly the Two Platoons of B Company were also withdrawn to SCHWABEN TRENCH. Excellent progress were made in consolidating the captured Trench and communication by the right flank communications was maintained. 20 P.M. there was no difficulty in keeping in touch. Between 5 P.M. and 7 P.M. on the 22nd inst both STUFF TRENCH and BAINBRIDGE TRENCH were heavily bombarded – later the same evening the Battalion was relieved by the 7th KING'S OWN – Relief being completed at 12:30 midnight and the Batt. moved to bivouacs in MARTINSART WOOD. The success of the Battalion were due to a large extent to the extraordinary accuracy of our artillery barrage which enabled	

T2134. Wt. W708–776. 500000. 4/15. Sir J. C. & S.

Army Form C. 2118.

WAR DIARY
or
INTELLIGENCE SUMMARY.
(Erase heading not required.)

Instructions regarding War Diaries and Intelligence Summaries are contained in F.S. Regs., Part II. and the Staff Manual respectively. Title pages will be prepared in manuscript.

Place	Date	Hour	Summary of Events and Information	Remarks and references to Appendices
STUFF TRENCH			Everything kept within 25 yds of the objective before the change lifted but the enemy Snipers from the Sunken Road of the First Company Grenadiers and two officers looked by the Machine Gun Support Gunners & fell. Our Casualties were not unduly heavy — Officers 2ⁿᵈ Lieut H.C. LANGDALE, M/lich BOX and 2ⁿᵈ Lieut WELLS were wounded. Other Ranks — Killed 23 Wounded 71 Missing 30. A large number of prisoners were taken by the Battalion. The Battalion rested and was completed with Equipment and on the 24th inst the battle of MARTINSART	
MARTINSART WOOD	23/10/16 24/10/16		were allotted to the Battalion.	
SCHWABEN REDOUBT	25/10/16		The Battalion relieved the 4/5ᵗʰ BLACK WATCH in the SCHWABEN REDOUBT — A and D Companies in the front line — B Company in Support and C Company in Reserve.	
	26/10/16		At dawn Enemy Counter attacked STUFF TRENCH on our right and were repulsed — no attack was made on our position although front line was heavily shelled.	
	27/10/16		The Battalion was relieved by the 17ᵗʰ KINGS ROYAL RIFLES and proceeded to NORTH BLUFFS — While in the position the Battalion had unwounded all its own ammunition and in addition 10 wounded of the BLACK WATCH and 2 of the KINGS ROYAL RIFLES.	
NORTH BLUFFS	28/10/16 29/10/16		The Battalion rested on the 28ᵗʰ inst. On the 29ᵗʰ inst the whole Battalion was detailed for digging reserve Trenches in THIEPVAL WOOD — B and C Companies by day and A and D by night.	
	30/10/16		The Battalion relieved the 1/6ᵗʰ CHESHIRE REGT in the LEFT RIVER SECTION — Relief completed at 1 p.m.	

Army Form C. 2118.

WAR DIARY
or
INTELLIGENCE SUMMARY.
(Erase heading not required.)

Instructions regarding War Diaries and Intelligence Summaries are contained in F. S. Regs., Part II. and the Staff Manual respectively. Title pages will be prepared in manuscript.

Place	Date	Hour	Summary of Events and Information	Remarks and references to Appendices
LEFT RIVER SECTION	30.10.16		B Company and Two Platoons of C Company in first line in Tunnels No 3 and 10 with other Platoons leaving free exits for 2nd & Tunnels — Two Platoons of C Company in Support and A and D Companies in Reserve in INNISKILLEN TRENCH. A very wet night which caused Trenches to fall in in several places.	
	31.10.16		A quiet day and a considerable amount of work done in repairing temporary Trenches.	
	1-11-16			

G.W. Drapper Lieut Col.
Commanding 13 Royal Sussex Regt.

Secret

O.O. Coys 13th Royal Sussex Regt.

The Battalion will assemble for assault as follows.
"B" Coy will assemble in three waves. The first wave will be in PIPE MINE or continuation of it on a frontage of (approx) 125 yds (not 75 yds as in O.O. order No 15.)
The men outside PIPE MINE must not be more than 50 yards in advance of BAINBRIDGE TRENCH.
The advance from SCHWABEN TRENCH will be made across the open by waves.
The waves will move in lines of sections in single file as far as BAINBRIDGE TRENCH.

The first They will enter this trench to move into PIPE MINE as beyond BAINBRIDGE TRENCH movement of formed bodies may be observed if visibility is good.
The first second wave will be just in front of BAINBRIDGE TRENCH & the 3rd wave just behind.

"C" Coy will move via ZOLLERN

TRENCH with the two platoons forming the 1st wave in front. From ZOLLERN TRENCH to BAINBRIDGE TRENCH the advance will be made across the open by waves, each wave being in line of sections in single file.

The first wave will crawl out from BAINBRIDGE TRENCH not further than 50 yards with its right in touch with the left of B Coy. The second wave will be just in front of BAINBRIDGE TRENCH and the third just behind. These movements will be completed by zero – 15 minutes without fail.

Two platoons of A Coy from WOOD POST will move to SCHWABEN TRENCH & take over half the position now occupied by B Coy. This movement to be completed by zero – 2 hours.

On completion of these movements at zero – 15 minutes the position of the Battalion will be as follows:

On completion of these movements, at zero – 15 minutes, the position of the Battalion will

be as follows:
B & C Coys in attack formation
in front & behind BAINBRIDGE
TRENCH.
2 platoons of D Coy in BAINBRIDGE
TRENCH
2 platoons of D Coy in SCHWABEN
TRENCH. Coy Hd Qrs HESSIAN
TRENCH.
2 platoons of A Coy in SCHWABEN
TRENCH
2 platoons of A Coy in dug outs in
THIEPVAL.
Coy Hd Qrs SCHWABEN TRENCH
35th Hd Qrs ZOLLERN TRENCH

H.W. Draffen Lt Col
Comdg 13th Royal
Sussex Regt

19/1/16.

116th Brigade.
39th Division.
66~~~~~~~~~~~~~

13th BATTALION

THE ROYAL SUSSEX REGIMENT

NOVEMBER 1916

D.9

WAR DIARY
or
INTELLIGENCE SUMMARY.
(Erase heading not required.)

13TH BATTN ROYAL SUSSEX REGT

Place	Date	Hour	Summary of Events and Information	Remarks and references to Appendices
PIONEER RD	1/11/16		The Battalion was relieved by the 11/6th Cheshire Regt. and moved to huts in PIONEER ROAD. Relief was reported complete by 2.15 p.m. New draft of 135 O.R. arrived for duty and were posted to coys as follows:– A Coy 30. B Coy 35. C Coy 40. D Coy 30. The draft for the most part came from the 5th and the 9th Bns R. Sussex Reg. and were a very satisfactory lot of men.	
	2/11/16		Battn moved to huts in MARTINSAART WOOD. Working party of 250 O.R. was supplied for work on the AUTHUILLE MOUQUET FERME RD. work proceeded satisfactorily till about 1.30 p.m when a hostile aeroplane flew over and shortly afterwards the road was shelled. Bn regrets the loss of 4 killed and 2 wounded. Working party returned to MARTINSAART WOOD about 5 p.m.	
	3/11/16.		Day spent in interior economy. Weather rapidly becoming worse and worse.	
	4/11/16		Heavy rain fell all day. Foot parades and medical inspections held.	
	5/11/16		The Bn relieved the 17th Notts and DERBY REGT. in the RIVER CENTRE section with B and C coys in the front line holding pts. 13, 95, 86, A7, 38 and 91, 8A, A5, 16 respectively with A and D coys in support and reserve in dug outs	

Army Form C. 2118.

WAR DIARY
or
INTELLIGENCE SUMMARY.
(Erase heading not required.)

Instructions regarding War Diaries and Intelligence Summaries are contained in F. S. Regs., Part II. and the Staff Manual respectively. Title pages will be prepared in manuscript.

Place	Date	Hour	Summary of Events and Information	Remarks and references to Appendices
RIVER CENTRE SECTION	5/11/16		about Bⁿ H.Q^s at point 29 (ref. map SCHWABEN REDOUBT EDITION 1/5000). The night passed quietly except for intermittent shelling in the region of p^{ts} 84, 47, and 29.	
	6/11/16.		The Battⁿ was relieved by the 17th NOTTS and DERBY REGT and returned to billets in MARTINSAART WOOD. Relief was reported complete 5.55 p.m. Total casualties for period of 24 hrs in the trenches:- 1 killed and 5 wounded. Captⁿ Story granted leave 8th to 17th 1916.	
MARTINSAART WOOD.	7/11/16		Day devoted to interior economy replacement of deficiencies of equipment etc. Captⁿ Story recalled from leave to give evidence in the case of 2/Lt A.K.A Gillow. Pte/Fry 9 O.R. reported for duty and were posted 15 C Coy. 7/11/16. Battⁿ supplies working parties totalling 2,550 O.R. to work under the supervision of the R.E. One party of 250 to work on THIEPVAL R.P. one party 50 to carry duck boards to PAISLEY DUMP. One party of 250 to work on THIEPVAL R.P. in the morning. Court of enquiry held on the accidental wounding of 2 R.A.M Chance.	
	8/11/16			
	9/11/16		Bⁿ supplied a working party of 250 O.R. for work on the THIEPVAL R.P. remainder of the Battⁿ used the baths at MARTINSAART. Weather improved considerably and a noticeably large no. of enemy aeroplanes reconnoitred our lines.	

T2134. Wt. W708—776. 500000. 4/15. Sir J. C. & S.

Army Form C. 2118.

WAR DIARY
or
INTELLIGENCE SUMMARY.
(Erase heading not required.)

Instructions regarding War Diaries and Intelligence Summaries are contained in F. S. Regs., Part II, and the Staff Manual respectively. Title pages will be prepared in manuscript.

Place	Date	Hour	Summary of Events and Information	Remarks and references to Appendices
MARTINSAART WOOD	9/11/16		Draft of 3 O.R reported for duty and were posted to B(1) and D coys (2)	
	10/11/16		The Battalion relieved the 1/6th Cheshires in the Brigade reserve in THIEPVAL. Small working parties supplied under R.E. supervision	
	11/11/16		Coys. employed on salvage, clearing of dug-outs and burying dead.	
	12/11/16		Batt⁵ relieved the 14th B⁷ Hampshire Reg⁷ in the RIVER CENTRE section and took up preparatory positions for the operation to be carried out by the Division. Relief was completed by 4 p.m.	
	13/11/16		During the night of the 12/13th Nov. the assaulting troops assembled in their battle positions without interference from the enemy. These were complete by 3 a.m. The duty of the battalion was to hold the line during the attack and to supply ammunition parties and general traffic control. At zero + 4 minutes the attacking troops carried their first objective with practically no opposition. For sometime afterwards the situation was obscure owing to a thick mist, which while rendering communication difficult materially aided operations by screening our troops from hostile artillery observation. 2ⁿᵈ Lt Wheatley sent out two patrols to ascertain the situation at about 8.30 a.m. These patrols on their return reported all objectives gained, but a small party	

Army Form C. 2118.

Instructions regarding War Diaries and Intelligence
Summaries are contained in F. S. Regs., Part II.
and the Staff Manual respectively. Title pages
will be prepared in manuscript.

WAR DIARY
or
INTELLIGENCE SUMMARY.
(Erase heading not required.)

Place	Date	Hour	Summary of Events and Information	Remarks and references to Appendices
THIEPVAL	13/11/16		of German machine gunners and snipers were holding out in NO MANS LAND. These however were soon cleared and shortly after 10 a.m. the work of consolidation was commenced on the newly captured ground. The casualties in the battalion were very slight and some excellent work was done by a volunteer stretcher party from A Coy. which evacuated 27 cases from NO MANS LAND, and also a fac another party that established a bomb stop from which the assaulting troops drew. From the large number of prisoners captured it was evident that the attack took the enemy completely by surprise, but from the no of regiments represented, it is more than probable that a relief was taking place at the time. The attack proved to be one of the most successful attacks of the "great Push" and was a fitting conclusion to the operations of the 39th Division on the SOMME.	
	13/11/16	5 p.m	The Battn was relieved by the Rifle Brigade and moved to dugouts in the SOUTH BLUFFS.	
	14/11/16		Orders received for the brigade to move to WARLOY. Coys marched off at 11.30 a.m and reached billets about 5.30 p.m. Weather became very cold with heavy	

T2134. Wt. W708-776. 500000. 4/15. Sir J. C. & 8.

Army Form C. 2118.

WAR DIARY
or
INTELLIGENCE SUMMARY.
(Erase heading not required.)

Instructions regarding War Diaries and Intelligence Summaries are contained in F. S. Regs., Part II. and the Staff Manual respectively. Title pages will be prepared in manuscript.

Place	Date	Hour	Summary of Events and Information	Remarks and references to Appendices
	15/11/16		Frosts at night time. The Battalion marched to billets in AUTHIEULLE on the outskirts of DOULLENS arriving there about 7.30 p.m. 2nd Lt S.J. DAVIS reported for duty and was posted to C Company.	
AUTHIEULLE	16/11/16		Day spent in billets.	
	17/11/16		Battalion entrained for HOPOUTRE at 11.50 p.m. Entraining station DOULLENS very cold journey with a small fall of snow during the night.	
	18/11/16		Train reached destination at 7.30 a.m. Battalion detrained and marched to "L" camp WATOU ROAD POPERINGHE arriving there about 10.30 a.m.	
"L" CAMP POPERINGHE	19/11/16		Day spent in cleaning up equipment and clothing inspections.	
	20/11/16		B Coy found working party of 100 O.R. for work on Z camp. remainder of companies carried on with the general cleaning up of equipment etc. Col Draffen departure leave.	
	21/11/16		Training commenced.	
	22/11/16		Training carried on.	
	23/11/16		ditto	

Army Form C. 2118.

WAR DIARY
or
INTELLIGENCE SUMMARY.
(Erase heading not required.)

Instructions regarding War Diaries and Intelligence Summaries are contained in F. S. Regs., Part II. and the Staff Manual respectively. Title pages will be prepared in manuscript.

Place	Date	Hour	Summary of Events and Information	Remarks and references to Appendices
L CAMP POPERINGHE	24/11/16		Test Inspection by the G.O.C. VIII Corps. Battalion formed up in close columns of companies in line on the parade ground in the centre of the camp. The Battalion was complimented on its turn out.	
"	25/11/16		Training in camp. No. 4242 Pte TITE executed. 2nd Lt KEOGH departed on Sniping Course.	
"	26/11/16		Church services held. Capt Robinson 2nd Lt Tierney went on Engineering Course.	
"	27/11/16		Route march for all the bans except C & D coys who trained.	
"	28/11/16		Training. Route march for C & D coys.	
"	29/11/16		Training. Battalion Officers' Mess inaugurated. Capt MacDougall nominated President	
"	30/11/16		Training.	

M Gardner Capt
for
Major Commdg 13th R. Sussex Regt

1.12.16.

116th Brigade.

39th Division.

13th BATTALION

THE ROYAL SUSSEX REGIMENT

DECEMBER 1, 9, 16.

War Diary
of
Lieutenant General Pope
from November to December 1916
Vol 10

D.10

Army Form C. 2118.

WAR DIARY
or
INTELLIGENCE SUMMARY.
(Erase heading not required.)

Instructions regarding War Diaries and Intelligence Summaries are contained in F. S. Regs., Part II. and the Staff Manual respectively. Title pages will be prepared in manuscript.

Place	Date	Hour	Summary of Events and Information	Remarks and references to Appendices
"L" CAMP POPERINGHE	1/12/16		Training	
	2.12.16		ditto. weather bad. Batt⁵ had a practise Turn-out at 10.p.m. all were ready to move off in 40 minutes. Col Draffen returned from leave.	
	3.12.16		Training — Turn-out repeated. Corps Commander inspected the camp during the luncheon hour.	
	4.12.16		Training. 2ⁿᵈ Lt S.J. DAVIS reported sick and was evacuated to hospital.	
	5.12.16		ditto. Two Officers returned for duty. Capt⁻ W.W. Fitzherbert 2.2.2.Lt N de P. MacRoberts. Capt⁻ Fitzherbert took over command of C. coy. 6.12.16 Lt MacRoberts was posted to A. Coy. The Batt⁵ was very glad to have these two officers back again. They had previously rendered valuable services.	
	6.12.16		Brigade Route march. Brigadier inspected en-route" by the Army Commander. Turn-out practise repeated. Time Taken 30 minutes.	
	7.12.16		2ⁿᵈ Lt Gellan left for the base having been dismissed the service by G.C.M. 2ⁿᵈ Lt L.K. RAYNER returned to the unit and was posted to B coy. Adjutant 2. O.C. C & D coys. reconnoitred the line to be taken over by the Battalion.	

Army Form C. 2118.

WAR DIARY
or
INTELLIGENCE SUMMARY.
(Erase heading not required.)

Instructions regarding War Diaries and Intelligence Summaries are contained in F. S. Regs., Part II. and the Staff Manual respectively. Title pages will be prepared in manuscript.

Place	Date	Hour	Summary of Events and Information	Remarks and references to Appendices
1 Camp POPERINGHE	8.12.16		Training. 2i/c and O.C. A & B coy reconnoitred the line. A coy. master was of the sergeant "M camp.	
"	9.12.16		Training — weather very bad. Battn allotted baths at COUTHOVE. A battalion concert was held in the recreation hut & was very much appreciated.	
"	10.12.16		Church Services held in the camp. Capt. H. Story departed on leave.	
"	11.12.16		The 116th Infantry Brigade relieved the 115th Inf. Brigade in the Right Section of the line commencing on the 11th Instant. The Battalion entrained at POPERINGHE at 4.15 p.m. for YPRES siding and detrained at 5.30 p.m. Guides from the 16th Welsh being at the Station. Guides led the coys. to dug-outs in the CANAL BANK and relief was reported complete at 7.30 p.m. B, C, 2 D coys were in dug-outs on the North Bank of the Canal and A in Tunnel dug-outs on the South side.	
	12.12.16		The Battalion relieved the 17th ROYAL WELSH FUSILIERS in the TURCO FARM Sector Relief was reported complete by all companies at 7.35 p.m. The following were the dispositions taken up by the Battalion:— A & B coys in the front line. This was held by means of 12 posts of 1 N.C.O and three men each the line being to all intents and purposes non-existent and	

WAR DIARY
or
INTELLIGENCE SUMMARY.
(Erase heading not required.)

Army Form C. 2118.

Place	Date	Hour	Summary of Events and Information	Remarks and references to Appendices
TURCO FARM	12.12.16		badly waterlogged. The remainder of a coy which was the night front company in CLIFFORD TOWERS with company headquarters at c.15.c.4.5. Support platoons of B coy in VICARS LANE - coy H.Qrs at c.20.b.35.60. Two companies in the neighbourhood of Battalion H.Qrs. with coy H.Qrs at c.20.d.45.45 and c.21.c.25.40. The line was normally held with 6 L.G. Posts by night and 5 by day one gun being withdrawn to CLIFFORD TOWERS. The condition of trenches was very bad the recent heavy rains having waterlogged the communication trenches and rendered drainage very difficult. The night passed very quietly and the total absence of rifle and machine gun fire was very noticeable. Lt Col F.G.W. DRAFFEN awarded the D.S.O. this award created great satisfaction in the battalion.	
	13.12.16		Day passed quietly. The enemy artillery was very inactive and our trenches and defences received no attention. During the night 2nd Lt MacRoberts took a fighting patrol into NO MAN'S LAND but encountered none of the enemy. The patrol returned to the our lines shortly after 11p.m.	
	14.12.16		Enemy showed slightly more activity and at about 12.30pm the WILLOWS	

INTELLIGENCE SUMMARY.

(Erase heading not required.)

Instructions regarding War Diaries and Intelligence Summaries are contained in F. S. Regs., Part II. and the Staff Manual respectively. Title pages will be prepared in manuscript.

Place	Date	Hour	Summary of Events and Information	Remarks and references to Appendices
TURCO F.M SECTION			received attention from a battery of "17" mm guns. During the night 2nd Lt R.S. CHALLIS took out a fighting patrol into NO MAN'S LAND but, as on the previous night none of the enemy were encountered. The going in NO MAN'S LAND was extremely bad and the ground for the greater part was under water. 2nd Lt MACROBERTS evacuated to hospital. The shortage of Officers was becoming a serious proposition and the loss of this officer was keenly felt.	
"	15.12.16		Enemy artillery again inactive. During the night Capt. FITZHERBERT took out a patrol to reconnoitre the sap at MORTELDJE Ft. The latter was found to be uninhabited, and the patrol returned about 11.30 p.m. At about 11 p.m. a German or Germans came across our wire and attempted to mark one of the posts. He was or they were fired at and retired.	
"	16.12.16		The Battn was relieved by the 11th R.S.R. Reg. and became the left Battn in support in dug-outs on the canal bank. Relief was reported complete at 7.15 p.m.	
	17.12.16		nightly working parties supplied for VICARS LANE and ATLAS dumps.	
	18.12.16		ditto "	

Army Form C. 2118.

WAR DIARY
or
INTELLIGENCE SUMMARY.
(Erase heading not required.)

Instructions regarding War Diaries and Intelligence Summaries are contained in F. S. Regs., Part II. and the Staff Manual respectively. Title pages will be prepared in manuscript.

Place	Date	Hour	Summary of Events and Information	Remarks and references to Appendices
CANAL BANK	19/12/16		Working parties supplied as for previous 3 days.	
	20/12/16		Capt. MACDOUGALL and 2nd Lt E.J. HARDEN went on leave. The Battalion relieved the 11th R.S.R in the HILLTOP SECTOR, which complete 7.30 p.m.	
HILLTOP FARM SECTION.	21/12/16		Our artillery carried out a heavy bombardment of the enemy trenches on the night of the Divisional front, otherwise which provoked a certain amount of retaliation. The Batt" regrets the loss of Lt CRISSBROOK Killed away valuable N.C.O. who has done goodwork. During the night Lt Sparks took out the 'usual' fighting patrol. no enemy were encountered.	
	22.12.16		Day passed quietly. During the night 2nd Lt HOLMWOOD carried out a reconnaissance of NO MAN'S LAND. Although none of the enemy were encountered there went several snipers and a hostile machine gun active. At about 2.30 a.m. the enemy opened a violent bombardment of the front line with TM's and shells of all calibers. No infantry action however took place, and very little damage was done. TURCO FARM received attention from minenwerfer, a large number of which failed to explode.	
	23.12.16		Quiet day owing to the weather. Artillerie of both sides inactive.	
	24.12.16		Battalion was relieved by the 11th HERTS. and marched to "G" camp A.16.d.7.9.	

Army Form C. 2118.

WAR DIARY
or
INTELLIGENCE SUMMARY.
(Erase heading not required.)

Instructions regarding War Diaries and Intelligence Summaries are contained in F. S. Regs., Part II. and the Staff Manual respectively. Title pages will be prepared in manuscript.

Place	Date	Hour	Summary of Events and Information	Remarks and references to Appendices
"G" CAMP POPERINGHE	24/12/16		Battalion arrived in camp about 10.30 p.m. D coy. suffered the loss of 2 men killed by shell fire in the WILLOWS shortly before relief.	
	25/12/16		Every effort was made to provide a suitable meal for the men on Christmas Day and the Christmas dinner was apparently a great success.	
	26/12/16		Training in camp.	
	27/12/16		ditto.	
	28/12/16		ditto.	
	29/12/16		ditto.	
BOESINGHE RESERVE.	30/12/16		The 116th Infantry Brigade relieved the 118th Brigade in the BOESINGHE section of the line. The Battalion moved into reserve in huts at B.13.A.1½.B. arriving there at 5.30 p.m. The accomodation was very limited and a few men were accomodated in the adjoining camp occupied by the 116th M.G. Coy. Coy. officers reconnoitred the line and the Battalion H.Qrs of the support and reserve battalions.	

H J Graham Capt.
Com-dg. 13th R. Sussex Regt.

Confidential Vol XI

Dr B Price Edwards Esq
New Bury
1876

Army Form C. 2118.

WAR DIARY
or
INTELLIGENCE SUMMARY.
(Erase heading not required.)

Instructions regarding War Diaries and Intelligence Summaries are contained in F. S. Regs., Part II. and the Staff Manual respectively. Title pages will be prepared in manuscript.

Place	Date	Hour	Summary of Events and Information	Remarks and references to Appendices
"M" camp.	1-1-17		Training. Working parties supplied for work on the line.	
	2-1-17		" Lt. Col. Doafen D.S.O and Major Heagerty	
			" Lt. Col. ___ W. P's supplied.	
	3-1-17.		left the battalion for 6-days at the VIII Corps.	
			Training — W. P's supplied.	
	4-1-17		The Battalion relieved the 14th Hants Reg. in the BOESINGHE support. The following	
			went the dispositions taken over. Batt. Headquarters at B.10 d.3.3.	
			C. Coy on the "A" line.	
	5-1-17		Working parties supplied for the front and immediate support lines	
			2nd Lt R.W. EVANS granted 10 days leave.	
	6-1-17.		Working parties supplied. Day very quiet.	
	7-1-17		" " In the afternoon the enemy carried out a	
			heavy bombardment of the Belgian front on the left with Trench mortars and	
			minnis.	
	8-1-17		The Batt. relieved the 14th Bn Hants. in the front line with A. B. & D. coys.	
			in the front line and C coy. in support. new batt. Headquarters	
			Batt. H.Q. at BOESINGHE CHATEAU. Owing to great enemy artillery	

Army Form C. 2118.

WAR DIARY
or
INTELLIGENCE SUMMARY.
(Erase heading not required.)

Instructions regarding War Diaries and Intelligence Summaries are contained in F. S. Regs., Part II. and the Staff Manual respectively. Title pages will be prepared in manuscript.

Place	Date	Hour	Summary of Events and Information	Remarks and references to Appendices
	8-1-17		Activity it was thought possible that he might be going to attempt a raid on our trenches and consequently great precautions were taken. However the night passed quietly and his bombardment was evidently retaliation for ours.	
	9-1-17		Day passed very quietly and a good deal of work was done on the line. Our snipers were active and claimed a victim.	
	10-1-17		Enemy minenwerfers very active and our artillery experienced great difficulty in silencing them. HUNTER STREET and BRIDGE STREET were badly knocked about but a large number of the minnies fell in between the front line and the VILLAGE LINE doing no damage. At about 11 p.m. an intense bombardment lasting ½ an hour started on the right flr divisional artillery apparently cooperating. A Trench was also carried out by the 55th Division with excellent results. 2nd Lt. E. BARTLETT granted 10 days leave.	
	11-1-17		The Battn was relieved by the 1/4th Hampshire Regt and moved to billets in BOESINGHE support Battn Headquarters at BLUET FARM.	

Army Form C. 2118.

WAR DIARY
or
INTELLIGENCE SUMMARY.
(Erase heading not required.)

Instructions regarding War Diaries and Intelligence Summaries are contained in F. S. Regs., Part II. and the Staff Manual respectively. Title pages will be prepared in manuscript.

Place	Date	Hour	Summary of Events and Information	Remarks and references to Appendices
BOESINGHE.	11-1-17		relief was reported complete by 10 p.m.	
	12-1-17		The usual working parties for the front line supplied. Weather suddenly became very cold and in the afternoon there was a heavy fall of snow. 5 O.R. reported for duty and were accordingly furnished toys.	
	13-1-17		Working parties supplied. Weather still bad.	
	14-1-17.		The Batt.n relieved the 14th Battalion Hampshire Reg.t in the front line. relief was reported complete by 9 p.m. Capt.n H.J. Booked admitted to hospital suffering from Laryngitis. 2nd Lieut Wood Bastled temporarily assumed the duties of adjutant.	
	15-1-17		Very heavy fall of snow during the night followed by a slow thaw with very difficult owing to the continual collapse of the trenches.	
	16-1-17		The Batt.n was relieved by the 16th Batt.n Royal Welsh Fusiliers Regiment on the evening of the 16th Instant. On relief the battalion moved to Billets in YPRES. The word taken was ELVERDINGHE – BRIELEN – YPRES. and the reported all in billets shortly before 1 a.m. The billets taken over were renovated by the 12th Batt.n	

Army Form C. 2118.

WAR DIARY
or
INTELLIGENCE SUMMARY.
(Erase heading not required.)

Instructions regarding War Diaries and Intelligence Summaries are contained in F.S. Regs., Part II. and the Staff Manual respectively. Title pages will be prepared in manuscript.

Place	Date	Hour	Summary of Events and Information	Remarks and references to Appendices
	16-1-17		Royal Sussex Regt and the Dispositions taken over were as follows :— Battn Headquarters opposite the BARRACKS, RUE DE NOTRE DAME., 2 Companies (B & C) in the RAMPARTS and 2 Companies (A & D) in the ECOLE on the YPRES – MENIN ROAD. Captn F.E. Wheatley granted 10 days leave.	
	17-1-17		Reconnoitring parties sent up to the line. Two new officers joined for duty 2nd Lt V.S. Cox and 2nd Lt G.W. Embledon with 3rd Battn Royal Sussex Regt. These officers were posted to C & D Coys. respectively.	
	18-1-17		Working parties supplied to the front line and for work in the support lines.	
	19-1-17		Ditto YPRES Square in the neighbourhood of the Cloth Hall was consistently shelled during the day in YPRES – POPERINGHE also receiving attention.	
	20-1-17		The Battn relieved the 12th Battn Royal Sussex Regt in the Right Sector RAILWAY WOOD SECTOR on the evening of the 20th. The relief was reported complete at 8.30 p.m. The following were the dispositions of the Battn	

Army Form C. 2118.

WAR DIARY
or
INTELLIGENCE SUMMARY.
(Erase heading not required.)

Instructions regarding War Diaries and Intelligence Summaries are contained in F. S. Regs., Part II. and the Staff Manual respectively. Title pages will be prepared in manuscript.

Place	Date	Hour	Summary of Events and Information	Remarks and references to Appendices
RAILWAY WOOD	20-1-17		C & D coys. in the front line with coy. Headquarters at I.12.c.65.20 and I.11.B.30.30 respectively. A & B coys in support in BEEK TRENCH and WEST LANE with coy. H.Q.s at I.11.c.70.66 and I.11.c.85.80 respectively. Battn Headquarters in SOUTH LANE I.10.d.55.60. The trenches generally speaking were in a very bad condition and, with the rapidly increasing activity of the German snipers, very dangerous. Approaches to the front line consisted of WEST LANE and MUD LANE the latter in parts being almost derelict.	
	21-1-17		Owing to the weak state of the unit 22 men per coy were employed in wiring nightly and considerable progress was made. During the day the enemy showed considerable artillery activity and our front was intermittently shelled all day. Our artillery retaliated vigorously.	
	22-1-17		Capt E.L. Du Moulin reported for duty and was posted to C coy. This officer was a regular soldier of Pigeon Service and came from the 1st Battn Royal Sussex Regt.	

Army Form C. 2118.

WAR DIARY
or
INTELLIGENCE SUMMARY.
(Erase heading not required.)

Instructions regarding War Diaries and Intelligence Summaries are contained in F. S. Regs., Part II. and the Staff Manual respectively. Title pages will be prepared in manuscript.

Place	Date	Hour	Summary of Events and Information	Remarks and references to Appendices
RAILWAY WOOD	23.1.17		Enemy artillery considerably more active and also his aircraft. Our aeroplanes drove off and Tarp driven down in our own lines. Support line communication trenches and wire shelled intermittently throughout the day. A great deal of R.E material was drawn & with the limit one Company dumps made. 10 more Jung Boxes had but no new store could be put out owing to frozen ground.	
	24.1.17		Enemy artillery appeared to be registering on Comm: trenches and support lines - very active throughout the day - his aeroplanes also were extremely active and approved 5 outclass our own. A very good day for observation. In the evening the Battalion was relieved by the 12th Batt. Royal Sussex Regt and moved to YPRES RAMPARTS and the ÉCOLE (Leaving Battalion in support to the Right RAILWAY WOOD Sector) Relief complete & from all in billets 9.30 p.m.	
	25.1.17		Into late morning at about 3 a.m. enemy about 30 Strong miked to delivery night trunk of F. left Battalion following after preliminary bombardment - our casualties were light but 2 men of 14 1/3 Bn Sussex Regt were missing. They left in ground and were dealt on buttongor which friend out to the 213 Bgde. Working parties on CAMBRIDGE TRENCH and HEDGE and HALF MOON TRENCHES were furnished.	

Army Form C. 2118.

WAR DIARY
or
INTELLIGENCE SUMMARY.
(Erase heading not required.)

Instructions regarding War Diaries and Intelligence Summaries are contained in F. S. Regs., Part II. and the Staff Manual respectively. Title pages will be prepared in manuscript.

Place	Date	Hour	Summary of Events and Information	Remarks and references to Appendices
RAILWAY WOOD	26.1.17		Enemy's artillery continued very active along the whole front - Working parties were provided for HEDGE and HALF MOON trenches. Burying party and improving fire bricks. Wiring etc. worked in CAMBRIDGE TRENCH.	
	27.1.17		Headquarters and D Company moved from YPRES to the ECOLE. Headquarters now being A.R. and D. Companies and Headquarters of ECOLE. C Company in the RAMPARTS YPRES. The MENIN ROAD was shelled between 9 and 10.30 a.m. at move than Completed by 11 a.m. move about 5h. Working parties provided as in previous days. Enemy D Company had one man wounded. artillery and aerial activity continued. 2 Lieut CHALLIS reported back to duty from sick leave.	
	28.1.17		The Batt. relieved the 12th Batt. Royal Sussex Regt. in the Right Sector RAILWAY WOOD SECTOR in the evening of 28th. The relief was reported complete at 8 p.m. The following were the dispositions of the Battn :- A & B Coys. in the front line with Coy Headquarters at I.12.c.65.20 and I.11.8.30.30 respectively. C & D coys in support in BEER TRENCH and WEST LANE with Coy. Hd. Qrs. at I.11.c.70.65 and I.11.C. 80.80 respectively. BATT. Hd. Qrs. in SOUTH LANE at I.10.d.55.60. 2/Lt Andrews and 2/Lt HOLMWOOD reported for duty from COURSES and rejoined "A" Coy. 2/Lt COUDREY reported for duty from GENERAL COURSE and rejoined "C" Coy.	

T2134. Wt. W708-776. 500000. 4/15. Sir J. C. & S.

Army Form C. 2118.

WAR DIARY
or
INTELLIGENCE SUMMARY.
(Erase heading not required.)

Instructions regarding War Diaries and Intelligence Summaries are contained in F.S. Regs., Part II. and the Staff Manual respectively. Title pages will be prepared in manuscript.

Place	Date	Hour	Summary of Events and Information	Remarks and references to Appendices
RAILWAY WOOD	29-1-17		ENEMY ARTILLERY active throughout the day especially on main communication trenches. His snipers also active. During the evening 500 EMERGENCY RATIONS taken up by trolley to BEEK TRENCH. and dump formed there close to junction of BEEK TRENCH and WEST LANE. 400 EMERGENCY RATIONS taken up to RAILWAY WOOD TUNNEL (LEFT FRONT COY. HD. Qrs.) and dump formed there. Wire (concertina) prepared by all Coys. in the trenches during the day, and put out in front during night.	
	30-1-17		BOMBARDMENT carried out by our artillery, including CORPS HEAVY ARTILLERY, of the enemy's front & support lines. Started at 8-45 a.m. & finished at 4 p.m. Enemy's artillery retaliated vigorously on our front & support lines. Also on our communication trenches especially WEST LANE and SOUTH LANE. Many shells fell near Batt. Hd. Qrs. One shell fell into OFFICERS' SERVANTS dug-out and wounded six of the Servants, five of them severely. Capt. COXHEAD hit slightly in the back during the morning. All were evacuated to Field Ambulance for treatment. During day 3 O.R's were killed and 10 O.R's each wounded. At 5.45 p.m. two strong fighting patrols of one officer and 30 O.R's under	

T2134. Wt. W708-776. 500000. 4/15. Sir J. C. & S.

Army Form C. 2118.

WAR DIARY
or
INTELLIGENCE SUMMARY.
(Erase heading not required.)

Instructions regarding War Diaries and Intelligence Summaries are contained in F. S. Regs., Part II. and the Staff Manual respectively. Title pages will be prepared in manuscript.

Place	Date	Hour	Summary of Events and Information	Remarks and references to Appendices
RAILWAY WOOD	30-1-17		2/Lts. COULDREY and ANDREWS respectively were sent out on LEFT FRONT COY'S front and RIGHT FRONT COY'S front also respectively to reconnoitre the enemy's line. Objects of the patrols were: (a) to discover damage done to enemy's wire by the bombardment. (b) to discover damage done to enemy's front line: (c) to enter enemy's front line and obtain an identification, also discover whether enemy was holding front line or not. RESULT OF PATROLS. Found that enemy wire was damaged but no definite gaps thro' which entry into his trenches could be made were found. Enemy holding his front line strongly. Enemy's front line did not appear to be extensively damaged. On return of patrols about 9-30 p.m. Lewis guns and Vickers guns opened continuous fire for rest of night and early morning on enemy wire to prevent him repairing damage.	
	31-1-17		ENEMY ARTILLERY very active during early morning especially shelling WEST LANE & SOUTH LANE near BATT. Hd. Qrs. About 9-30 a.m. a shell near B.H.Qrs. wounded Lt. Col. DRAFFEN, D.S.O., Major HEAGERTY and Reg. Sgt. Major R.S. SLADE. All were evacuated and Major Heagerty who had been hit in the back died of his wounds at No. 2 Canadian Hosp. later in the day. This was a terrible blow to the Batt. and his loss is greatly felt by all ranks.	

Army Form C. 2118.

WAR DIARY
or
INTELLIGENCE SUMMARY.
(Erase heading not required.)

Place	Date	Hour	Summary of Events and Information	Remarks and references to Appendices
RAILWAY WOOD	31-1-17		During afternoon Bn. Hd. Qrs. moved up to BEEK TRENCH for the night in accordance with Brigade instructions. This became ENEMY ARTILLERY appeared to have Bn. Hd. Qrs. in SOUTH LANE well taped. disposition of new Bn. Hd. Qrs. — I.11.C.80-80.	

HdWheeler. Capt.
Commanding 13R. R. Sussex Regt
3-2-17

Franklin

Vol 17

War Diary

2nd Bn Royal Sussex Regt

Vol XII

D.12

Army Form C. 2118.

WAR DIARY
or
INTELLIGENCE SUMMARY.
(Erase heading not required.)

Instructions regarding War Diaries and Intelligence Summaries are contained in F. S. Regs., Part II. and the Staff Manual respectively. Title pages will be prepared in manuscript.

Place	Date	Hour	Summary of Events and Information	Remarks and references to Appendices
RAILWAY WOOD	1-2-17		About 5 a.m. the ENEMY opened an intense ARTILLERY and MINNENWERFER BOMBARDMENT on RIGHT FRONT COY. of BATT. on our Left Front, 14th Bn. HANTS Reg. Enemy's intention was to raid but owing to prompt action of Capt. GOLDSMITH, 14th Bn. HANTS Reg. this was frustrated. During the day enemy artillery was quiet. In the evening the Batt. was relieved by 12th R. Sussex Reg. and proceeded to the billets they had just vacated. A, C & D Coys. & Bn. Hd. Qrs. to the ECOLE. "B" Coy. to the RAMPARTS. Relief was carried out smoothly and without casualties.	
	2-2-17		"A" Coy. provided working party during the day in clearing and arranging EMERGENCY RATIONS etc. in X line. B, C & D Coys. carried out training in billets. "A" Coy. provided working party during night and carried up and put out 101 coils barbed wire in front of X line.	
	3-2-17		"A" Coy. provided working party to complete work commenced in X line on 2nd. Feb. B, C & D Coys. In the evening Battalion was relieved at the ECOLE by the 12th R. Sussex Reg. with the exception of D. Coy. The latter Company had to be left behind without rations and without blankets as no orders had been received in time to prevent these being sent on by the Transport. The battalion proceeded

Army Form C. 2118.

WAR DIARY
or
INTELLIGENCE SUMMARY.
(Erase heading not required.)

Instructions regarding War Diaries and Intelligence Summaries are contained in F. S. Regs., Part II. and the Staff Manual respectively. Title pages will be prepared in manuscript.

Place	Date	Hour	Summary of Events and Information	Remarks and references to Appendices
RAILWAY WOOD	3-2-17		by rail from YPRES ASYLUM to BRANDHOECK SIDING, and marched from there to "O" Camp at A.30.6.2.1, arriving at the Camp by 2 a.m. on 4-2-17.	
"O" Camp.	4-2-17		First day in "O" Camp. General "clean-up" of person, equipment, rifles etc. "D" Coy. was relieved in the evening at the ECOLE, YPRES, and arrived by rail via BRANDHOECK SIDING about 10 p.m. Capt. F.L. du MOULIN now in command of Battalion. Capt. Coxhead returned for duty and became 2nd. in command.	
	5-2-17		TRAINING in Camp. Lt. A.C. TAYLER reported for duty, and was posted to "D" Coy.	
	6-2-17		do. Reconnoitring to front line by officers, N.C.O's and runners, via KEMMEL BEKE.	
	7-2-17		do. do.	
	8-2-17		do. do.	
	9-2-17		do. do.	
	10-2-17		do. do.	
	11-2-17		CHURCH PARADE.	
	12-2-17		TRAINING in Camp. Capt. F.L. du MOULIN proceeded on a GRENADE COURSE. Capt. Coxhead assumed command of the Battalion.	
	13-2-17		TRAINING in Camp.	

Army Form C. 2118.

WAR DIARY
or
INTELLIGENCE SUMMARY.
(Erase heading not required.)

Instructions regarding War Diaries and Intelligence Summaries are contained in F. S. Regs., Part II. and the Staff Manual respectively. Title pages will be prepared in manuscript.

Place	Date	Hour	Summary of Events and Information	Remarks and references to Appendices
"O" Camp	14-2-17		TRAINING IN CAMP.	
	15-2-17		Battalion relieved at "O" Camp by 2/5th Lancashire Fusiliers. On relief battalion marched to POPERINGHE CHEESEMARKET STATION where it entrained for MERCKEGHEM by train vicinal to BOLLEZEELE & from there by route march to MERCKEGHEM. Battalion now in Corps Rest in billets.	
	16-2-17		General "clean up", kit inspection etc., and cleaning of billets	
	17-2-17		TRAINING.	
	18-2-17		CHURCH PARADE	
	19-2-17		TRAINING. Lt. E. SPARKS, 2/Lt. N. de L. MacRoberts & 2/Lt. W. VIETH, reported for duty & were posted to B, A and D Coys. respectively. Capt. F.L. du Molin returned to the Bath & assumed command	
	20-2-17		do. Recreational training in the afternoon.	
	21-2-17		do.	
	22-2-17		do.	
	23-2-17		do.	
	24-2-17		Battalion entrained at BOLLEZEELE and travelled by train vicinal to the CHEESE MARKET STATION POPERINGHE. On arrival Batt'n marched to ST LAWRENCE CAMP T.30.c. the 116th F. Brigade becoming the Brigade in Corps Reserve.	

Army Form C. 2118.

WAR DIARY
or
INTELLIGENCE SUMMARY.
(Erase heading not required.)

Instructions regarding War Diaries and Intelligence Summaries are contained in F. S. Regs., Part II. and the Staff Manual respectively. Title pages will be prepared in manuscript.

Place	Date	Hour	Summary of Events and Information	Remarks and references to Appendices
ST. LAWRENCE CAMP	24-2-17		Lt Col Drysen D.S.O. returned from sick leave and resumed command of the Battalion.	
	25-2-17		The Battalion relieved the 9th Yorkshire Regt. in the Right Section OBSERVATORY RIDGE sector taking over the following dispositions B C & D Coys in the front line from night 15 left with A Coy in support in HALIFAX TRENCH and Batt. Headquarters at RUDKIN H.Q. I.24.c ½.1½. The relief was a long one and was not reported complete till 1 a.m. The general condition of the line was not good and supply arrangements necessitated large carrying parties.	
	26-2-17		Owing to poor visibility the Artilleries of both sides were inactive and except for desultory firing on a few points the day passed quickly. During the night our patrols were active but encountered no resistance.	
	27-2-17		Day again passed quietly. During the morning the enemy fired about 20 5.9's on RUDKIN H.Q. slightly damaging the trench but causing no casualties.	
	28-2-17		The Batt was relieved by the 12th Bn R. Sussex Regt. Shortly after relief had been reported complete. Bombing started on the night of the batt. front and almost immediately an intense bombardment with artillery and trench mortars was opened on our front. Telephone communication being cut the situation was very	

T2134. Wt. W708–776. 500000. 4/16. Sir J. C. & S.

WAR DIARY
or
INTELLIGENCE SUMMARY.

(Erase heading not required.)

Army Form C. 2118.

Place	Date	Hour	Summary of Events and Information	Remarks and references to Appendices
	28.2.17		absence but it appears that no infantry action took place. Fortunately the Battⁿ was just clear of the trenches and no casualties occurred, but the right coy. of the 12ᵗʰ suffered a certain number. The bombardment died down and finally ceased at about 10.50 p.m. 2ⁿᵈ Lts. DOBBIE, LAWRENCE and SOANO reported for duty and were taken on the strength of the Battⁿ.	
	1-3-17.		Lt. Col. Emery. 13ᵗʰ R. Sussex Regᵗ.	

Confidential

War Diary
of
3rd Dn. Lucknow Reg.
March 1914.

Vol 13

D.13

Army Form C. 2118.

WAR DIARY
or
INTELLIGENCE SUMMARY.
(Erase heading not required.)

Instructions regarding War Diaries and Intelligence Summaries are contained in F. S. Regs., Part II. and the Staff Manual respectively. Title pages will be prepared in manuscript.

Place	Date	Hour	Summary of Events and Information	Remarks and references to Appendices
OBSERVATORY RIDGE SECTOR THE BUND	1-3-17		Battalion now the Battalion in Support in OBSERVATORY RIDGE SECTOR. DAY occupied in cleaning, inspections etc. "A" Coy in MAPLE COPSE, "B" Coy in the REDAN, "C" & "D" Coys in the BUND	
"	2-3-17		Day passed quietly. During the afternoon enemy shelled YPRES, paying special attention to the LILLE GATE. Visibility good. Many hostile aeroplanes up.	
"	3-3-17		Battalion relieved by 4/15th BLACK WATCH, and proceeded by march route to YPRES ASYLUM, where it entrained for ST. LAWRENCE CAMP via BRANDHOEK siding. Relief passed off without hitch, and the whole battalion was in Camp by 4 a.m. on 4th.	
ST. LAWRENCE CAMP	4-3-17		Men rested. No work done. Rev. FROSSARD C.F. having joined 116th Infantry Brigade for duty, became attached to the Battalion.	
"	5-3-17		Battalion went to Divisional Baths. Training commenced under Company arrangements.	
"	6-3-17		Training in Camp.	
"	7-3-17		do.	
"	8-3-17		do.	

Army Form C. 2118.

WAR DIARY
or
INTELLIGENCE SUMMARY.
(Erase heading not required.)

Instructions regarding War Diaries and Intelligence Summaries are contained in F. S. Regs., Part II. and the Staff Manual respectively. Title pages will be prepared in manuscript.

Place	Date	Hour	Summary of Events and Information	Remarks and references to Appendices
ST. LAWRENCE CAMP.	9-3-17		Battalion relieved 4/5th BLACK WATCH in OBSERVATORY RIDGE SECTOR, and became Right Front Battalion of RIGHT BRIGADE again. ST. LAWRENCE CAMP was left at 5-15 p.m., entrainment at BRANDHOECK SIDING was accomplished successfully. As railway line near YPRES had been broken in several places by shell fire, Battalion disentrained some way from the ASYLUM and marched from there up the line. Relief was complete about 3 a.m. on 10th.	
OBSERVATORY RIDGE SECTOR	10-3-17		First day passed quietly. Enemy put a few shells over MAPLE COPSE and on the NEW TRENCH being constructed in ARMAGH WOOD to link up STAFFORD TRENCH with HALIFAX TRENCH. Visibility poor. No aeroplanes up.	
"	11-3-17		Visibility good. Many aeroplanes up both hostile and our own. Superiority of the Hun plane very marked today. Two of our aeroplanes brought down, one near RAILWAY WOOD and one in the MOAT, YPRES. Observer seen to fall out of the latter plane before it reached the ground. Six enemy aeroplanes patrolled our front line in the evening about 5 p.m. Artillery on both sides active during the whole day at intervals on back areas. Night all quiet.	
"	12-3-17		Enemy very active during early morning with rifle grenades and egg bombs on the	

WAR DIARY or INTELLIGENCE SUMMARY

Army Form C. 2118.

Place	Date	Hour	Summary of Events and Information	Remarks and references to Appendices
OBSERVATORY RIDGE SECTION	12-3-16		right and left Company fronts. Our heavy Trench Mortars registered in the afternoon. This produced heavy retaliation from enemy "minnies" and rifle grenades. Very slight damage was done to left & Centre Coy. Fronts. Parapet was damaged in several places & Sap was blocked. Working parties during the night repaired all this damage. No casualties were suffered.	
" "	13-3-16		Morning passed without incident. About 1 p.m. enemy again started on left Coy. front with "minnies". Artillery retaliation was asked for. This was given on HUN front & support line and he was almost immediately silenced. Our heavy Trench Mortars registered on the left Battalion front about 3-30 p.m. Enemy again vigorously retaliated putting shrapnel "minnies" and H.E. on the left Coy front for about half an hour. Our artillery was again asked for retaliation, which they gave, once more successfully silencing the enemy. During the night the Battalion was relieved by 12th R Sussex Regt. Relief was complete at 10-30 p.m. Battalion then became Battalion in Brigade Reserve and took up dispositions as follows:- Bn. Hd Qrs. and "D" Coy. in Cellars at KRUISSTRAAT (H.18.d); "C" Coy. in Crosley Barracks, YPRES; "A" & "B" Coys. in THE BUND.	

Army Form C. 2118.

WAR DIARY
or
INTELLIGENCE SUMMARY.
(Erase heading not required.)

Instructions regarding War Diaries and Intelligence Summaries are contained in F. S. Regs., Part II. and the Staff Manual respectively. Title pages will be prepared in manuscript.

Place	Date	Hour	Summary of Events and Information	Remarks and references to Appendices
KRUISSTRAAT	14-3-17		Battalion rested during day. Every available man employed on WORKING PARTIES up the line during the night, in accordance with Divisional Scheme. "C" & "D" Coys. bathed in the morning.	
"	15-3-17		NIGHT WORKING PARTIES again found. Enemy shelled YPRES slightly in the afternoon.	
"	16-3-17		Do. do. Lieut. Col. DRAFFEN, D.S.O. took command of 118th Inf. Brigade in place of Brigadier-General Hornby who went to Hospital Sick. Capt. F. L. du MOULIN assumed command of Battn.	
"	17-3-17		Battalion relieved 12th Bn. Royal Sussex Reg. in OBSERVATORY RIDGE SECTOR on night of 17th/18th, and became RIGHT FRONT BATT. of RIGHT BRIGADE. Dispositions of Coys. on relief were as follows – "B" Coy. – Right-front Coy.; "C" Coy. – Centre front Coy.; "D" Coy. – Left-front Coy. "A" Coy. – Support Coy. in HALIFAX ST. Relief was carried out very quietly, and was complete at 11 p.m. Capt. F. L. du MOULIN granted permission to wear the badges of rank of Major while acting 2 i/c Battalion.	
OBSERVATORY RIDGE SECTOR	18-3-17		Enemy artillery fairly active all day. Shrapnel & H.E. put over on our left-front Coy. (D. Coy.) about 10 a.m. Our artillery were asked to retaliate. This they did & effectually silenced the enemy guns. Nothing of importance occurred during rest of the day.	
"	19-3-17		Enemy artillery quiet during the night 18/19th. A few rounds fired by a single gun into ZILLEBEKE VILLAGE in the early morning. Visibility poor owing to heavy clouds and rain.	

WAR DIARY
or
INTELLIGENCE SUMMARY.
(Erase heading not required.)

Army Form C. 2118.

Instructions regarding War Diaries and Intelligence Summaries are contained in F. S. Regs., Part II. and the Staff Manual respectively. Title pages will be prepared in manuscript.

Place	Date	Hour	Summary of Events and Information	Remarks and references to Appendices
OBSERVATORY RIDGE SECTOR 29/1/17			Visibility still poor. No aeroplanes up. Some artillery activity on our right front during the morning. In the afternoon the enemy severely shelled the centre of B company front. Probably the bomb in at second point, but inflicting no casualties. From the post that our wire was cut, a raid was anticipated. A Lewis gun & Lewis gun detachment stand at this point, but no attempt movement of the enemy was detected. Unlucky shells from B company exploded in rear of the trench & the following morning 4 Enemy artillery very active on back areas own advance posts who reported 2 very heavy bombardment a little passing the Bund. Later in the evening the enemy put several rounds of T&R H.E. Shells and Lacrymatory Shells around a district hit on A.T.D Dugs, roadhouse completely smashed at Ieterete at that moment only 1 man was inside, he was killed instantaneously. Our artillery paid no compulsory transport which had been observed from our left W. D'lougy with lavish it will. The enemy activity was answered by our own artillery. The enemy was scarcely able to some very severe shelling. The battalion was relieved during the night by the 1st Cheshires proceeding to the Asylum Station at Ypres where it entrained for Brandhoek marched into Lil Lawrence Camp at 11 a.m. and next the Brigade than became Group Reserve	
	2/2/17			

T2134. Wt. W708—776. 500000. 4/15. Sir J. C. & S.

Army Form C. 2118.

WAR DIARY
or
INTELLIGENCE SUMMARY.
(Erase heading not required.)

Instructions regarding War Diaries and Intelligence Summaries are contained in F. S. Regs., Part II. and the Staff Manual respectively. Title pages will be prepared in manuscript.

Place	Date	Hour	Summary of Events and Information	Remarks and references to Appendices
ST LAWRENCE CAMP	24/3/17		Men rested. Cloud obscuring ap was dark.	
	25/3/17		Training in camp during the morning. In the afternoon football matches were arranged.	
	26/3/17		Training in camp during the morning. In the afternoon football matches were arranged. Major de Mulin whilst watching a demonstration at Pouringhs of wrestling with airplanes made an ascent, but unfortunately after the machine had risen about 100 feet it crashed to the ground, pinning him the pilot beneath its debris. Accidence was as quickly forthcoming tho' Major de Mulin was extricated. He was suffering from concussion and also from a wound in the head. He was removed to No. 10 C.C.S. He left [illegible] accoured [illegible] command of the Battalion during his absence. Church Parade. The service was conducted by Capt [illegible].	
	27/3/17		Training in camp. Lt [illegible] de P. Washburn granted authority to wear badge of rank of Captain, which commanding a Company. A football match between the Officers & Sergeants resulted in a win for the Officers. Score 4–0. A very successful concert was held in the evening at the [illegible] A.S.C. [Hut?]	
	28/3/17		Training in camp.	
	29/3/17		Training in camp. Battalion relieved [illegible] Battalion in OBSERVATORY RIDGE SECTOR, and	

WAR DIARY
or
INTELLIGENCE SUMMARY
(Erase heading not required.)

Army Form C. 2118.

Place	Date	Hour	Summary of Events and Information	Remarks and references to Appendices
ST. LAWRENCE CAMP	28/3/17		Became Right Support Battalion of Right Brigade. Entrainment took place at BRANDHOEK SIDING. No. 3 SIDING near BRANDHOEK. Entrainment near the ASYLUM was completed by 9.15. the battalion marched from station to its dispositions on the line as follows:—	
OBSERVATORY RIDGE			to STAFFORD ST — B Company on the BUND. — A Company 2 Platoon in MAPLE COPSE 2 Platoon in THE REDAN. D Company in the BUND. Steady work on the BUND. Right Coy was completed at 2.30 a.m. attempt a casualty A HUDGKISS returned to duty. who an officer and two other ranks reported sick from fatigue, reported sick outside offer. B Company on STAFFORD TRENCH were subjected to steady counter-attack by enemy. C Company was (namely) directed at RYDKIN HOUSE. Bn Battalion Headquarters which were however in two places. Only one casualty resulted. There was some shelling	
	29/3/17		out Ypres. Machinery fire was active Officer of all Companies During the morning there was considerable shelling on the duckboards between the BUND & YPRES. and particularly around the HALF GATE between the afternoon the enemy shelled the BUND on our left. 2 or 3 aeroplanes came over the BUND during the evening.	
	31/3/17		The Batt. relieved the 12th R. Sussex Reg. and became Right Front Battalion. Relief took place without "incident". Disposition of Companies were as follows :— Three Coys.	

Army Form C. 2118.

WAR DIARY
or
INTELLIGENCE SUMMARY.
(Erase heading not required.)

Instructions regarding War Diaries and Intelligence Summaries are contained in F. S. Regs., Part II. and the Staff Manual respectively. Title pages will be prepared in manuscript.

Place	Date	Hour	Summary of Events and Information	Remarks and references to Appendices
OBSERVATORY RIDGE.	31/1/17		were in the front line "B", "A", and "D", reading from right to left. "C" Coy. was in Support in HALIFAX ST. Batt. Hd. Qrs. were in RUDKIN HOUSE. The night was quiet. Three of the enemy entered STEWART SAP, on the left of "A" Coy. front, during the night, and one of them shot at our Sentry with his revolver, wounding him in the neck. The wounded Sentry grappled with the BOSCHE, but could not hold him. All three got away, leaving behind them one cap as identification.	

[signature] Capt.
Comdg. 13th R. Sussex Reg.

1-4-17.

Confidential Vol 14

D.14

War Diary
of
3rd Dn R Sussex R
for
April 1917

WAR DIARY or INTELLIGENCE SUMMARY

Army Form C. 2118.

(Erase heading not required.)

Place	Date	Hour	Summary of Events and Information	Remarks and references to Appendices
OBSERVATORY RIDGE	1/4/17		During the afternoon our artillery carried on a heavy bombardment of the enemy front support lines, during which our own front line was cleared. The enemy retaliation was fierce, no casualties were sustained. In the morning the enemy had been shelling MAPLE COPSE with 8" Howitzers.	
	2/4/17		Our artillery again bombarded enemy lines, particularly at Hill 60 our right. Later in the evening snow began to fall heavily & 2 or 3 our entries noticed 2 men in white overalls leave the enemy line. One of our snipers went out into No Mans Land fired on them hitting one, whereupon the other fled.	
	3/4/17		A blizzard raged for several hours, our firing 9-12mm. dyer in front. Later this gave place to brilliant sunshine, the snow melted rapidly causing a considerable amount of water in the trenches, obviated a lot of work in trenches. Our snipers were active obtained 2 victims. Enemy aeroplanes patrolled the front line for long periods without molestation except from our Lewis Guns which fired several rounds but without success.	
	4/4/17		About 11am the enemy became active with Rifle Grenades on B company front, in order to direct the retaliating fire. 2/Lt. H.C. KEOGH got on the fire step for that only time. as a few moments when hit through the head killed by a sniper.	

T2134. Wt. W705-776. 500000. 4/15. Sir J. C. & S.

Army Form C. 2118.

WAR DIARY
or
INTELLIGENCE SUMMARY.
(Erase heading not required.)

Place	Date	Hour	Summary of Events and Information	Remarks and references to Appendices
OBSERVATORY RIDGE	4/4/17		The Battalion was relieved by the 1/8th London Regt & became in Brigade Reserve. A & C Companies in the BUND. B & D in YPRES.	
YPRES	5/4/17		The Battalion supplied working parties.	
	6/4/17		Battalion relieved by 1/16 Batt. & 1/5 Essex Regt. marched back to ST LAWRENCE CAMP arriving at 4 a.m.	
ST LAWRENCE CAMP	7/4/17		Paraded for Church Parade. EASTER SUNDAY. The Battalion Band conducted by Band Sgt. Mead paraded under Regimental arrangements. In Church S.O. the C.O. in the afternoon. 9 officers & 9 Divisional Nominates. Maj. Gen. G. J. Cuthbert C.B., C.M.G. The weather turned out intensely cold, even falling of sleet etc. No G. 61 was received. Men of the whole as very pleased until the Battalion Platoons were paraded under the new Laader Councils Section of Lewis of new Lewis Gunners. With knowledge of the air it was held on the evening at which it was happy to without acidity. The Battalion entered at ok 3 Brigade worked hungry arrangements.	
	8/4/17		Leaving at 9.4 for billets at ASKUM STATION meads from the sea MENIN ROAD entered the 166 RIFLE BRIGADE on the front line at HOOGE sector. A & C Companies in front line B & O in supports. Weather still intensely cold & snow falling very heavily.	

Army Form C. 2118.

WAR DIARY
or
INTELLIGENCE SUMMARY.
(Erase heading not required.)

Instructions regarding War Diaries and Intelligence Summaries are contained in F. S. Regs., Part II. and the Staff Manual respectively. Title pages will be prepared in manuscript.

Place	Date	Hour	Summary of Events and Information	Remarks and references to Appendices
HOOGE	12/4/17		to England front line was heavily shelled throughout at several points the casualties.	
CRATER	13/4/17		Enemy shelled our support reserve lines throughout the day owing to change of the weather to be taking advantage of the good visibility he regular weather very poor. Artilleries of both sides quiet. The Enemy fired a few short on his usual targets shortly after dark.	
	14/4/17		The Battalion was relieved in the HOOGE SECTOR by the 10th Batt. Northumberland Fusiliers 23rd Division. The relief was carried out satisfactorily but was interrupted by a short period owing to a strafe on the Ypr Divisional front for which the enemy retaliated slightly on the MENIN ROAD. On relief the Battalion entrained for No. 3 siding and on arrival marched to ST. LAWRENCE CAMP.	
	15/4/17		Day spent in camp.	
	16/4/17		The Batt. relieved the 11/10th Liverpool Scottish in the right support, HILL TOP SECTION taking over dug outs on the CANAL BANK. The relief was carried out satisfactorily and without a hitch.	
	17/4/17		Training continued on the CANAL BANK. Officers reconnoitred the right battalion front.	

Army Form C. 2118.

WAR DIARY
or
INTELLIGENCE SUMMARY.
(Erase heading not required.)

Instructions regarding War Diaries and Intelligence Summaries are contained in F. S. Regs., Part II. and the Staff Manual respectively. Title pages will be prepared in manuscript.

Place	Date	Hour	Summary of Events and Information	Remarks and references to Appendices
MILL TOP.	18-4-17		The battalion regrets the loss of 2nd Lt. L.K. RAYNER killed by a shell while reconnoitring. His loss will be keenly felt as he was universally popular and was one of the original members of the Batt. when the Battn. came over seas. His body was buried at VLAMERTINGHE cemetery on the morning of the 19th.	
	19-4-17.		Training continued with working parties supplied for front line system nightly.	
	20-4-17.		The Brigadier General commanding the Brigade returned from hospital and Lt. Col. Drysdale rejoined the battalion. Six new officers reported for duty and were posted 15 boys. 15 under. 2nd Lt. R.H.P. BENNET 2nd Lt. W.J. BARNES to A Coy. 2nd Lt. BRANSON V.C. 2nd Lt. LANGDON to D Coy. 2nd Lt. CHAIZE J.F. to B Coy. 2nd Lt. HERRON R.M. to C Coy.	
	21-4-17.		Officers reconnoitred the left left (114th) Brigade front and the left sub right brigade front. ———— Training on CANAL BANK.	
	22-4-17.		Training and working parties.	
	23-4-17.		The battalion relieved the 12th Batt. R.S.R. in the front line Coys. taking over the following dispositions. B coy. 2 platoons in the front line and 2 platoons	

Army Form C. 2118.

WAR DIARY
or
INTELLIGENCE SUMMARY.
(Erase heading not required.)

Instructions regarding War Diaries and Intelligence Summaries are contained in F.S. Regs., Part II. and the Staff Manual respectively. Title pages will be prepared in manuscript.

Place	Date	Hour	Summary of Events and Information	Remarks and references to Appendices
HILL 70.	23-4-17		in BILGE TRENCH. Coy. Headquarters BILGE TRENCH. D. Coy. — two platoons in the front line, 2 platoons in TOWER TRENCH. C — Coy 1 two platoons in the x line one platoon in TOWER TRENCH. Coy H.Q. X line. — A coy 2 platoons in WILSON FARM. one platoon in X line and one platoon attached to the Bn front line coys. owing to lack of accommodation. Bn. HQrs in A x line Battn. Headquarters situated at LA BRIQUE.	
	24-4-17		Very considerable aerial activity owing to the clearness of the day. Shelling chiefly confined to back areas and batteries. Our artillery shelled left battalion front drawing considerable retaliation. At about 9.45 p.m. the enemy opened a barrage on the Division on our right and in response to the SOS our artillery replied immediately (the enemy sent up red and green rockets) right round the salient and the artillery of both sides vigorously replied bombards the opposing trenches. Strafe lasted for about three quarters of an hour during which time 2/Lt Cox and Sgt. BARLEY were both wounded the latter sustaining a broken leg.	
	25-4-17		A much quieter day our artillery continued wire-cutting on the left battalion front and also bombarded strong points behind his lines. Retaliation was again	

Army Form C. 2118.

WAR DIARY
or
INTELLIGENCE SUMMARY.
(Erase heading not required.)

Instructions regarding War Diaries and Intelligence Summaries are contained in F. S. Regs., Part II. and the Staff Manual respectively. Title pages will be prepared in manuscript.

Place	Date	Hour	Summary of Events and Information	Remarks and references to Appendices
HILL TOP	25-4-17	—	considerably but was chiefly confined to "minnies".	
"	26-4-17		A quiet day. Desultory shelling on the usual targets in the front systems. Rather noticeable increase in counterbattery work. Aeroplane activity very great, numerous undecisive encounters between large formations.	
	27-4-17		A very quiet day. Owing to mistiness artilleries of both sides were inactive and except for a few 5.9's in the neighbourhood of HILL TOP FARM no shooting was done. Fires in the tresche line were seen on two successive nights. A relief was expected owing to the but it appeared to be grass and straw burning. The origin was unknown inactivity of machine guns.	
	28-4-17		The Battalion was relieved in the line by the 1/3rd Cheshire Reg.t moving back by train to POPERINGHE and thence by route march to "L" camp.	
	29-4-17		Return of winter clothing. 2nd Lt WALTER O.G. reported for duty and was posted to D coy. (28-4-17)	
	30-4-17		Training in camp.	

G.b. Drapper Lt Col Comdg
13th R Sussex Reg.t
30-4-17.

Army Form C. 2118.

13 R Sussex
9/1/5

WAR DIARY
or
INTELLIGENCE SUMMARY.
(Erase heading not required.)

Instructions regarding War Diaries and Intelligence Summaries are contained in F. S. Regs., Part II. and the Staff Manual respectively. Title pages will be prepared in manuscript.

D.15

Place	Date	Hour	Summary of Events and Information	Remarks and references to Appendices.
BOUZELINGHAM TRAINING AREA	1.5.17		The Battalion moved by route march to ABEELE STN. and to WIPPENHOEK STN. where it entrained for ST. OMER. From thus the Battalion marched to billets in ST. MARTIN-AU-LAERT for the night on route for BOUZELINGHAM TRAINING AREA. The move was accomplished satisfactorily without incident.	
	2.5.17		The Battalion left billets in ST. MARTIN-AU-LAERT and entrained by route march to the TRAINING AREA via ZOUAUSQUE and BOISDINGHEM. Billets, which were as follows, were reached at 10.30 a.m. B. Coy and Battn. Headquarters were at QUERCAMP: A Coy, at la WATTINE: C and D Coys at NORTBECOURT.	
	3.5.17		Training in "C" Area commenced.	
	4.5.17		do.	
	5.5.17		Inspection of Battalion by Surgeon-General of 2nd Army. Rest of day was holiday.	
	6.5.17		Training continued on "C" Range. 2/Lt. H.T. Triggs returned from 10 days leave.	
	7.5.17		do.	
	8.5.17		Brigade Tactical Exercise.	
	9.5.17		do. Battalion Sports held in the afternoon. The following names of the Battalion appear in the G.O.C. in C.'s despatch: Lieut. Col. I.G.H. DRAFFEN D.S.O., T/Lieut. H.E. JONES, T/Lieut. A.B. WHEATLEY	
	10.5.17		Training continued	

Army Form C. 2118.

WAR DIARY
or
INTELLIGENCE SUMMARY.
(Erase heading not required.)

Instructions regarding War Diaries and Intelligence Summaries are contained in F. S. Regs., Part II. and the Staff Manual respectively. Title pages will be prepared in manuscript.

Place	Date	Hour	Summary of Events and Information	Remarks and references to Appendices
BOUVELINGHEM	11-5-17		Training continued. Brigade Tactical Exercise at which the Army Commander was present.	
TRAINING AREA	12-5-17		Training continued.	
	13-5-17		Church Parades were held at QUERCAMP and NORTBECOURT.	
	14-5-17		The Brigadier General Commanding inspected the Battalion at QUERCAMP and NORTBECOURT.	
	15-5-17		The Battalion moved by route march en route for the WORMHOUDT AREA and billeted for the night at ST. MARTIN-AU-LAERT.	
ST. MARTIN AU LAERT			and billeted there for the night.	
BUYSSCHEURE	16-5-17		The Battalion proceeded to BUYSSCHEURE by route march, where it marched with the Brigade to WORMHOUDT.	
WORMHOUDT	17-5-17		The Battalion proceeded to ARNEKE by route march, where it marched with the Brigade to WORMHOUDT and was billeted.	
	18-5-17		The Battalion visited the Divisional Baths and training was also carried out under Company arrangements.	
	19-5-17		Training continued under Company arrangements. 2nd Lieut. H.I. WHITE reported for duty and was posted to "D" Coy. The Rev. MURRAY M.W. C.F. having joined the 115th Infantry Brigade for duty was attached to this Battalion.	
	20-5-17		The Battalion took part in a BRIGADE CHURCH PARADE. 2nd Lieut. A.W. RICHARDSON reported for duty and was attached to "C" Coy.	
	21-5-17		Parades were under Coy. arrangements.	
	22-5-17		The Brigadier General Commanding inspected B Company, the remaining Coys. paraded under Company arrangements. Lieut. F. St. A. DAVIES reported for duty and was posted to B Company. The Rev. E.L. GROSSARD, having joined several units	

F. St. A. DAVIES reported for duty and was posted to B company. The Rev. E.L. GROSSARD, having joined several units

T-134. Wt. W708—776. 500000. 4/15. Sir J. C. & S.

Army Form C. 2118.

WAR DIARY
or
INTELLIGENCE SUMMARY.
(Erase heading not required.)

Instructions regarding War Diaries and Intelligence Summaries are contained in F. S. Regs., Part II. and the Staff Manual respectively. Title pages will be prepared in manuscript.

Place	Date	Hour	Summary of Events and Information	Remarks and references to Appendices
WORMHOUDT.	22.5.17 (continued)		ceased to be attached to this Battalion.	
	23.5.17		Training was continued.	
	24.5.17		do.	
	25.5.17		The Battalion continued training	
	26.5.17		The Brigadier General Commanding inspected Companies of this Battalion.	
	27.5.17		The Battalion attended Church Parade.	
	28.5.17		Training was continued	
	29.5.17		The Battalion moved by route march from WORMHOUDT and proceeded to "C" Camp.	
	30.5.17		Training was continued in Camp.	
	31.5.17		Training was continued. The Battalion moved up to the line and relieved the 14th K.R.R. on CANAL BANK.	

Lt Col Commanding
1st Bn The Royal Sussex Regt

Original

Army Form C. 2118.

13 R Sussex Regt

6/16

WAR DIARY
or
INTELLIGENCE SUMMARY.
(Erase heading not required.)

Army Form C. 2118.

Instructions regarding War Diaries and Intelligence Summaries are contained in F. S. Regs., Part II. and the Staff Manual respectively. Title pages will be prepared in manuscript.

D.16

Place	Date	Hour	Summary of Events and Information	Remarks and references to Appendices
CANAL BANK	1.6.17		The Battn. occupied the same billets as in April but under very different weather conditions. The Officers reconnoitred the front line and the companies provided several working parties.	
	2.6.17		Another beautiful day. The Battn. visited the Baths. The artillery action on both sides has been fairly continuous. Nieuport suffered its first casualties since the battalion came overseas.	
	3.6.17		Sunday. Church services were held in the chapels on CANAL BANK. At 11pm gas started to drift up the CANAL, it continued to grow stronger and at 1 am men were warned. Gas helmets were worn till about 3 a.m. by which time all the gas had cleared the theatre. There was a mixture of Lachrymatory and asphyxiating gases. There were no casualties though the gas was v. [?]	
	4.6.17		At night three companies went up Threadneedle Street to dig a new communication trench from THREADNEEDLE STR. to DURHAM TR.	
LA BRIQUE	5.6.17		The 13th Royal Sussex Regt. was relieved by us at LA BRIQUE. During the morning one of the snipers who had one in a blanco of the Battn. was killed in pointing to the enemy. The enemy artillery was very active. On the night of the 6/7th few casualties were occupied in improving ARMITAGE TR. and in making dugouts.	
	6.6.17			

Army Form C. 2118.

WAR DIARY
or
INTELLIGENCE SUMMARY.
(Erase heading not required.)

Instructions regarding War Diaries and Intelligence Summaries are contained in F. S. Regs., Part II. and the Staff Manual respectively. Title pages will be prepared in manuscript.

Place	Date	Hour	Summary of Events and Information	Remarks and references to Appendices
IN BRIQUE	7.6.17	At 3.10 a.m.	The Southern Army attacked WYSCHAETE. — The 39th Division made a demonstration along its front in order to distract the enemy's attention. The Battalion's part in the demonstration was as follows: — Dummies were placed in ARMITAGE TR. overnight and smoke bombs were ready to be discharged along the line, as the wind was not favourable the smoke bombs were not used. At zero hour two mines exploded away to our right; and at the same moment our artillery and machine guns opened on the enemy's first line. The enemy retaliated promptly on our first lines and communication trenches; the bombardment lasted forty minutes and when the artillery fire slackened, counter battery work ensued. The situation was quiet at six a.m. In the evening a fighting patrol of one officer and twenty other ranks was sent out beyond the screen of the working parties in ARMYTAGE TR. Four casualties were reported today. The Brigade on our left gave a demonstration with Gas. The hostile artillery was very active over CAVAN & BILGE TR.	
	8.6.17			
	9.6.17.		Hostile Artillery shelled the support lines in the vicinity of IRISH FM. Casualties today, fourteen were wounded of whom two died in hospital.	

T.J134. Wt. W708—776. 500000. 4/15. Sir J. C. & S.

Army Form C. 2118.

WAR DIARY
or
INTELLIGENCE SUMMARY.
(Erase heading not required.)

Instructions regarding War Diaries and Intelligence Summaries are contained in F. S. Regs., Part II. and the Staff Manual respectively. Title pages will be prepared in manuscript.

Place	Date	Hour	Summary of Events and Information	Remarks and references to Appendices
LA BRIQUE	10:6:17		The hostile artillery registered on LA BRIQUE with black shrapnel, and during the day shelled IRISH Fm. frequently with 5.9's. There were four more casualties today making a total of two killed, two died of wounds and twenty-seven wounded since the battalion came into the line. At midnight the battalion was relieved by the 12th Bn. Royal Sussex Regt.	
CANAL BANK.	11:6:17		The battalion occupied the same dugouts as previously – at the SOUTH end of the BANK. The company commanders were sent to reconnoitre the trenches for the work to be done to-night. Large working parties went up the line to-night to work on the new trenches and to carry up R.E. material. As one of these parties left, HERRON was wounded; he was sent immediately to the Advance Dressing Station in the BANK, and evacuated to the 2nd CANADIAN C.C.S. at POPERINGHE.	
	12:6:17		There were several welcome showers to-day. The company carried out an trench training during the day. We heard the sad news that 2nd/Lieut. HERRON, R.F. has died of his wounds; he was only just issued as IRISH with C.C.S.	
	13:6:17		We have now had nine casualties since the Battalion left LA BRIQUE; they have been almost entirely on the wiring-parties which have been furnished every night. To-night T/Capt. A.C. TAYLER was wounded whilst bringing his men home from their nights work.	

Army Form C. 2118.

WAR DIARY
or
INTELLIGENCE SUMMARY.
(Erase heading not required.)

Place	Date	Hour	Summary of Events and Information	Remarks and references to Appendices
CANAL BANK	13.6.17		He was in command of "A" Coy and was actually leading them when a shell burst in front of him; he was evacuated straightaway from the A.D.S. to 3rd CANADIAN C.C.S. He has since lost the lower half of his right leg and the doctors state that had he been another hour before receiving medical aid he would have died from loss of blood.	
	14.6.17		The Companies carried out another hour of training during the day. 2nd Lieut CHARLIS on being classified PERMANENT BASE owing to weak eyesight is struck off the battalion strength. Training was carried out as yesterday.	
	15.6.17		Officers nearest to accommodate the line.	
	16.6.17		Advance-parties were sent into the line during the afternoon and straight the Battalion relieved the 16th Bn. of the Rifle Brigade in the LANCASHIRE Fm. subsector, and became attached to the 117th Infantry Brigade. The 116th Infantry Brigade less this battalion retired to the CAMPS along the POPERINGHE - VLAMERTINGHE Road. The casualties since we entered the line on the 2nd are 48 by now.	
LANCASHIRE FM	17.6.17		A draft of 14 O.Rs. joined the Battalion. 2nd Lieut HOLLINGHAM O.W. reported for duty and is attached to the Battalion. The casualties to-day number 16.	
	18.6.17		At night carrying parties were provided and during the day was employed near FOCH Fm. Hostile artillery shelled HALIFAX STR., HEADINGLEY LANE and	

T.134. Wt. W708-776. 500000. 4/15. Sir J. C. & S.

Army Form C. 2118.

WAR DIARY
or
INTELLIGENCE SUMMARY.
(Erase heading not required.)

Place	Date	Hour	Summary of Events and Information	Remarks and references to Appendices
LANCASHIRE FM	18:6:17		LANCASHIRE FM, and in several cases obtained direct hits. Five men were wounded to-day and one killed.	
	19:6:17		Three men wounded to-day on the working party.	
	20:6:17		Eleven more casualties. The trench is in a very poor condition in parts of the front line here and the artillery bombards the support and communication trenches frequently.	
	21:6:17		Seven casualties. An Advance party was set forward to "B" Cur: of the Battn. The Battalion was relieved by 1/5 GORDON HIGHLANDERS and proceeded to "O" Camp where it spent the night.	
"O" Camp.	22:6:17		The Battalion entrained at POPERINGHE Main line Station at 12:30 p.m. and arrived at WATTEN at 4:40 p.m. Thence they marched to HOULLE, where they billeted. The remainder of the 116th Infantry Brigade arrived here from Camp two days previously. A draft of 45 men was posted to the battalion and joined for duty here.	
HOULLE.	24:6:17		A Church Parade was held for the Battalion by the Rev. M.W. MURRAY, C.F. The total casualties since June 2nd are : 1 Officer died of wounds, 1 officer wounded, eleven other ranks killed, six others ranks who died of wounds and eighty-five wounded.	
	25:6:17		Training of specialists was carried out during the day, and the battalion also went to range.	

T.1134. Wt. W708–776. 500000. 4/16. Sir J. C. & S.

Army Form C. 2118.

WAR DIARY
or
INTELLIGENCE SUMMARY.
(Erase heading not required.)

Instructions regarding War Diaries and Intelligence Summaries are contained in F. S. Regs., Part II. and the Staff Manual respectively. Title pages will be prepared in manuscript.

Place	Date	Hour	Summary of Events and Information	Remarks and references to Appendices
HOULLE	26.6.17.		The Battalion left Mentilles at noon and reached from one to seven p.m. O Battalion attack was carried out on the village of NORTEULINGHEM.	
	27.6.17.		The morning was spent in Training am from 6.30 to 11 p.m. and an attack was launched at the MILL in Area X 3. In the evening the officers attended a lecture on "MUSKETRY" by the officers of the Brigade	
	28.6.17		The Battalion shot at the range and carried out training scheme. At 5 p.m. LIEUT GEN. Sir IVOR MAXSE, K.C.B., C.V.O., D.S.O. lectured to the officers of the brigade on the lessons to be learnt from the Advance at Arras.	
	29.6.17		The Battalion was occupied during the day is digging model trenches. In the afternoon two officers per company and two N.C.O.s per platoon attended a demonstration by the Second (Army) Musketry School of a Company in the attack.	
	30.6.17		The Battalion was allotted the Baths during the day. Owing to the rain the brigade gymkhana was postponed.	

J.P. Duffus Lt Col
Commanding 13th Royal Surrey Regt

WAR DIARY
or
INTELLIGENCE SUMMARY.
(Erase heading not required.)

Army Form C. 2118.

11/8/21 13 R.R. Sussex Vol 17

Place	Date	Hour	Summary of Events and Information	Remarks and references to Appendices
BLUVILLE	1.7.17		In the morning the 12th and 13th Battalions attended Church Parade in a field close to our billets. In the afternoon the 13th Battn worked on the Practice Trenches. These trenches are a replica of the enemy lines on the 39th Divisional front but are dug only two feet deep; they are intended to give an idea of direction and distance in the forthcoming attack.	
	2.7.17		The Battalion again dug the Practice Trenches, principally those in the vicinity of Kitcheners Wood repeated on the ground by a line of laths. Lt-Col. Draffen D.S.O. left the Battalion this day to proceed to Aldershot for a course of instruction to Commanding Officers. He has commanded this Battn since it was in training in England. Major Coxhead M.C. assumed Command of the Battalion.	
	3.7.17		Specialist training was carried out during the day and in the evening the Platoon Commanders and N.C.O.s reconnoitred the Practice Trenches. Lieut. E. St Hill Davies was struck off the strength of the Battn. having been transferred to England – sick.	
	4.7.17		The Company Commanders took their Companies over the Practice Trenches and carried out an exercise in the despatch of messages. The Batts. of Coy. were clothed to take	

D.17

WAR DIARY or INTELLIGENCE SUMMARY

Army Form C. 2118.

Place	Date	Hour	Summary of Events and Information	Remarks and references to Appendices
HOYLLE	4.7.17		Battalion. 2nd Lieut W.J. BERNES having been transferred to England sick - is struck off the strength dated as 16.6.17.	
	5.7.17		The Batts were again platted to Ris Battalion. In the afternoon the Companies fired on the range close to 1st Brigade. Lieut. Col. J.H. LEVEY 2nd Gordon Highlanders took over the Command of this Battn. from Major Corkhead	
	6.7.17		The Battn worked on the Practice Trenches and afterwards carried out a scheme demonstrating an advance under Artillery fire.	
	7.7.17		The Battn. assembled behind BLUE TR. and attacked S. JULIEN across the Practice Trenches. Later the Companies practised some of the half-day trenches and then marched home to the Brigade funchara.	
	8.7.17		SUNDAY. The Assistant Chaplain General the Rev NEVILLE TALBOT officiated at a Church Parade held for the 12th and 13th Battalions. Lieut. D.C. ELPHICKE and Lieut. F.E.O. COUCHMAN there struck off the Establishment dated as 30.6.17.	

Army Form C. 2118.

WAR DIARY
or
INTELLIGENCE SUMMARY.
(Erase heading not required.)

Instructions regarding War Diaries and Intelligence Summaries are contained in F. S. Regs., Part II. and the Staff Manual respectively. Title pages will be prepared in manuscript.

Place	Date	Hour	Summary of Events and Information	Remarks and references to Appendices
HOULLE	8.7.17		SECOND LIEUT. C.V. EMBLETON was struck off establishment dated as 30.6.17.	
	9.7.17		The Brigade carried out an attack across the Practice Trenches. Officers commanding Companies detached their men on the training ground.	
	10.7.17		There was a second Brigade Attack today, particular attention being paid to intercommunication and liaison.	
	11.7.17			
	12.7.17		Four hours training was carried out by the Companies in the vicinity of their billets, from 2p.m. to 5p.m. were "Silent Hours" during which the men took compulsory rest prior to the night's operations. SECOND LIEUT. V.C. de GAELLE joined for duty and was posted to "B" Coy. At 11.30p.m. the Companies met at on the CALAIS ROAD at the top of MOULLE HILL & thence Key marched by CORMETTE and LEULINE to the Practice Trenches. A hot meal was issued to the men on their way. Zero hour. At 4.10 a.m the Attack commenced and before midday the Batt. was conducting its fullest objective – the line beyond S. JULIEN.	
	13.7.17			
	14.7.17		This day a Divisional Practice was carried out – zero hour being at 11 a.m.	
	15.7.17		The Commanding Officer held a Conference in the village-school for all those in	

Army Form C. 2118.

WAR DIARY
or
INTELLIGENCE SUMMARY.
(Erase heading not required.)

Instructions regarding War Diaries and Intelligence Summaries are contained in F. S. Regs., Part II. and the Staff Manual respectively. Title pages will be prepared in manuscript.

Place	Date	Hour	Summary of Events and Information	Remarks and references to Appendices
HOOGE	15.7.17		Changed Companies and Platoons in the attack with the 7th Batt. Church Parade was held as usual with the 7th Batt.	
	16.7.17		The Batt. left HOOGE at 12.30 pm and proceeded by train from WATTEN to HO POUTRE SIDING arriving at Z Camp at about 1 am 17/7/17. The camp was at the time partially occupied by the 5th Batt. of the Royal Sussex Regt. who proceeded at 10 a.m. to CANAL BANK. This is the first time the Battalion have not been on the SOMME.	
Z CAMP	17.7.17			
	18.7.17		The morning was divided between Battalion drill and the training of specialists. Special attention was paid to the instruction of the new draft in gas drill. Second Lieut. G. J. MARTIN returned from leave and was posted to "B" Coy. Second Lieut. G. F. SOANO was struck off strength on being transferred to the R.F.C. Parades were held in Camp as yesterday. During the day two parties paraded by me to inspect the model trenches at the A 30 Group Camps.	
	19.7.17			
A 30 GROUP CAMP.	20-21.7.17		The next two days were spent as the 19th.	
	22.7.17		SUNDAY The Battalion paraded for a route march to the A 30 Group Camps and on arrival took over as Tent and Billets Camp adjacent to "C" Camp.	

WAR DIARY
or
INTELLIGENCE SUMMARY.
(Erase heading not required.)

Army Form C. 2118.

Instructions regarding War Diaries and Intelligence Summaries are contained in F. S. Regs., Part II. and the Staff Manual respectively. Title pages will be prepared in manuscript.

Place	Date	Hour	Summary of Events and Information	Remarks and references to Appendices
	22.7.17		The evening a party was sent up the line to carry T.M. ammunition. Two or three	
A30 & RAVP			parts were killed and one wounded — the first casualties since the Battn. left	
CAMP			Flanders in June.	
	23.7.17		The Officers is go into action during the advance and the N.C.O.s in charge of	
			platoons held a conference at the Model near "C" Camp with the Officers. The	
			TANK SECTION working in conjunction with us on Z day	
			Company Commanders accompanied Bde. Trench Mortar during the afternoon and	
	24.7.17		an officer from each Company reconnoitred the QUEEN'S ROAD and a Covering PARTY	
			made by day and night.	
	25.4.17		The Battn. was found to CANAL BANK ROAD in 2 days arms parties. The	
			Officer & two M.Gun Companies in the attack went to support with the officers	
			of the 1/10 Liverpool Scottish who will advance on our right	
	26.7.17		The Commanding Officer held a Conference with Company Officers on the matter	
			of attack & the Instructions of H.H. Infantry Brigade issued regarding all	
	21.7.17		(At 1.30 p.m. the Yorks & Lancs & 118th Infantry Brigade issued instructions	
			Battalions to be ready to move at 5 p.m. ...	

WAR DIARY or INTELLIGENCE SUMMARY.

Army Form C. 2118.

(Erase heading not required.)

Instructions regarding War Diaries and Intelligence Summaries are contained in F. S. Regs., Part II. and the Staff Manual respectively. Title pages will be prepared in manuscript.

Place	Date	Hour	Summary of Events and Information	Remarks and references to Appendices
A30 Camp	27/7/17		Took over from the 52nd Siege Bty and the new site at A30 Camp.	
Camp			Re NIGHTENER SYSTEM. Orders to be more fully studied to ensure perfect readiness.	
	28/7/17		Books turned in and the officers' orders were issued. No further orders were received to-day and the Battalion remained in a state of complete readiness.	
			Orders were received to send an advance party to take over dugouts in CANAL BANK. Brigade Headquarters moved up to the CANAL. At about 10.30 p.m. hostile aeroplanes flew over and traversed the road outside the camp with M.G. fire. There were no casualties.	
	29/7/17 "X" day		At 8.30 p.m. the Battalion moved up to the CANAL BANK dugouts.	
CANAL BANK	30/7/17 "Y" day		At 9.30 p.m. the Bty proceeded to occupy its advancing position before attacking and by 2.50 a.m. to 3 a.m. for 1st July were registered to Rec. Hd. Place the Bn knd ammunition, and even to be in promised to have ready to move off.	
Advanced Trenches	31/7/17 Z day		At 3.50 a.m. the advance opened and at 5.33 a.m. the bty began to Cap. Ld. explored the Branch Line — at 8 a.m. A Coy supported by B Coy had taken the St. Julien to Contalmaison in the forward German line.	

J. M. Lees
Commd. 13th Siege Bn.

Army Form C. 2118.

13 R Sussex X 1501
V 6 1 8

WAR DIARY
or
INTELLIGENCE SUMMARY.
(Erase heading not required.)

Place	Date	Hour	Summary of Events and Information	Remarks and references to Appendices
ST. JULIEN and BLACK LINE	1-8-17		During the night 31st. July / 1st. Aug. the BOSCHE was very active with his artillery, heavily shelling the positions we had captured from him on the 31st. JULY especially the line of trenches known as the BLACK LINE (Canopus Trench) and our main line of defence which we had dug in front of it - about 150 yds - known as the dotted BLACK LINE. Bn. Hd. Qrs were established in CANOPUS TR. B and C Coys were firmly established in the dotted BLACK LINE while A and D Coys who were only about 70 O.R's strong and two officers were in ST. JULIEN VILLAGE. Rain commenced to fall heavily about 3 p.m. on 31st JULY and the ground was saturated. Both the BLACK LINE and the dotted BLACK LINE was full of water in places. No-one had had any sleep - everyone was wet through, but all were cheery and confident. About 12-30 a.m. on the morning of the 2nd August orders were received for all posts to be withdrawn from ST. JULIEN as our artillery	D 1

Army Form C. 2118.

WAR DIARY
or
INTELLIGENCE SUMMARY.
(Erase heading not required.)

Instructions regarding War Diaries and Intelligence Summaries are contained in F. S. Regs., Part. II. and the Staff Manual respectively. Title pages will be prepared in manuscript.

Place	Date	Hour	Summary of Events and Information	Remarks and references to Appendices
ST. JULIEN and BLACK LINE	1-8-17		were going to shell it. This was incomprehensible to us at the time, as with the exception of a few BOSCHE snipers in a ruined house some 300 yds. on the ST. JULIEN - POEL CAPELLE Rd, on the far side of the village none of the enemy were visible, nor were they in close proximity, according to reports by our advanced patrols. The village was re-occupied by us at 8 a.m. without incident and was held by the Battalion throughout the rest of the time until handed over on relief. Four Field Guns were captured by "A" Coy., and two machine guns in ST. JULIEN. Bn. H. Qrs. moved to	
	2-8-17		VANHEULE F.M. about 10 a.m. The Q.M. brought up rations in the morning on pack transport, and everyone was much comforted by these and a good issue of rum. The night passed quiet, so far as enemy movement was concerned, but artillery activity on both sides was tremendous. The BOSCHE shelled our new positions	

WAR DIARY
or
INTELLIGENCE SUMMARY.
(Erase heading not required.)

Army Form C. 2118.

Place	Date	Hour	Summary of Events and Information	Remarks and references to Appendices
ST. JULIEN and BLACK LINE	2.8.17		unceasingly, and it was during this period that most of our casualties were sustained. The rain meanwhile continued to render our trenches more and more uninhabitable and the men were forced to get out of them & lie on top. In the afternoon at about 4 pm the enemy went reported to be massing for counter-attack N.E. of ST JULIEN but this came to nothing. Indeed it was practically impossible for anyone to move owing to mud. On the night 2nd/3rd the 16th Sherwood Foresters came up to relieve the battalion. This was completed by 3 a.m. on the morning of 3rd in a particularly heavy barrage which the enemy put up on Vanheule Farm, CHEDDAR VILLA and across the WIELTJE - ST JULIEN Rd. The Bn. proceeded on relief to accommodation on the CANAL BANK.	

Army Form C. 2118.

WAR DIARY
or
INTELLIGENCE SUMMARY.
(Erase heading not required.)

Instructions regarding War Diaries and Intelligence Summaries are contained in F. S. Regs., Part II and the Staff Manual respectively. Title pages will be prepared in manuscript.

Place	Date	Hour	Summary of Events and Information	Remarks and references to Appendices
CANAL BANK	3-8-17		Battalion spent the day resting in dugouts	
SCHOOL CAMP	4-8-17		moved by rail from YPRES to POPERINGHE, thence by route march to SCHOOL CAMP	
	5-8-17		Cleaning & refitting in camp. Enemy aircraft dropped bombs in neighbourhood during evening & were fired on by A.A. Guns. No damage. 6 B.Other Ranks	
	6-8-17		Re-organisation continued. Battalion received a visit from the Corps Commander Lt. Gen. Sir I. Maxse, who thanked the Officers & O.R.s for what they had done in the push of July 31st.	
	7-8-17		Day spent refitting & re-organising at Battalion.	
PICHBOOM	8-8-17		Battalion left SCHOOL CAMP by route march to HOPOUTRE railway sidings. By rail to CAESTRE & motor lorry to PICHBOOM. During night enemy aircraft dropped bombs & fires M.G. in district. Engines to A.A. Guns.	
	9-8-17		Brigade inspected by the Divisional Commander Maj. Gen. C.G. Cuthbert, who thanked the troops for their work on July 31st-Aug 2nd. Lt. Col. J.H. Lorey Gordon Highlanders left the Battalion to take up the duties of Commandant of the XVIII Corps School.	

A6945 Wt. W14422/M160 350,000 12/16 D.D. & L. Forms/C./2118/14.

Army Form C. 2118.

WAR DIARY
or
INTELLIGENCE SUMMARY.
(Erase heading not required.)

Instructions regarding War Diaries and Intelligence Summaries are contained in F.S. Regs., Part II. and the Staff Manual respectively. Title pages will be prepared in manuscript.

Place	Date	Hour	Summary of Events and Information	Remarks and references to Appendices
P.CH.BOIS	9.8.17		Major H.T.K. Robinson D.S.O. from the 12th Royal Sussex assumed command. 2nd Lt. G.C. Taylor joined the Battalion & was posted to D Coy.	
	10.8.17		The Brigade was inspected by the commander of the 2nd Army, Maj. Gen. Sir H. Plumer.	
	11.8.17		The day was spent by the Companies refitting & reorganizing	
RIDGEWOOD	12.8.17		Brigade moves from the METEREN area, travelling by motor lorries to HALLEBLAST & thence by march to RIDGE WOOD CAMP. Lieut Steel R.A.M.C. has been posted as Medical Officer to this Battalion vice Capt. D.J. MacDougall wounded, as from 3/8/17.	
BOIS CONFLUENT	13.8.17		Enemy plane dropped a bomb on camp, killing two & wounding six members of the M.G.C. Battalion moves to BOIS CONFLUENT and became Battalion in reserve in the HOLLEBEKE sector. Casualties in the push of July 31st - Aug 2nd amounted to 14 officers & 250 O.R.	
BOIS CONFLUENT	14.8.17		Day spent repairing & renovating dug-outs & trenches. O.C. Coys with N.C.O.s made a reconnaissance of the front line. Quiet day	

Army Form C. 2118.

WAR DIARY
or
INTELLIGENCE SUMMARY.
(Erase heading not required.)

Instructions regarding War Diaries and Intelligence Summaries are contained in F. S. Regs., Part II. and the Staff Manual respectively. Title pages will be prepared in manuscript.

Place	Date	Hour	Summary of Events and Information	Remarks and references to Appendices
BOIS CONFLUENT	15/8/17		Working parties engaged renovating & improving dugouts. Salvage dumps formed. Enemy put some 5.9 before carry into road in rear. Enemy evening. Burry night working parties engaged on making mule track between FIXHOF FM	
	16/8/17		HOLLEBEKE, making a dump of wire & timber carrying. Officer recommended HOLLEBEKE SECTOR. Cox works in trench improvement.)	
	17/8/17		The Battalion relieves the 13th Bn. Royal Sussex in the right sub sector. HOLLEBEKE SECTOR on night of 17/18. The relief was carried out with no casualties.	
HOLLEBEKE SECTOR	18/8/17		Front line & supports OPTIC TRENCH shelled intermittently SPOIL BANK & OAK DUMP received attention during the night. No movement visible during day, all watering & work done during night.	
	19/8/17		Battalion H.Q. received attention from 4.2 & 5.9. Otherwise situation quiet. The G.S.O.I. Lt Col COSSETT R.F.A. visited Bn. H.Q. & obtained line cop. carried out patrols & found useful information.	
	20/8/17		Major Gen. G. J. Cuthbert C.B. C.M.G. gave up the command of the 39th Division. It was Major Gen. E. Freebern C.B. C.M.G. During night our artillery put	

A6945 Wt. W14422/M1160 350,000 12/16 D. D. & L. Forms/C./2118/14

WAR DIARY or INTELLIGENCE SUMMARY.

Army Form C. 2118.

(Erase heading not required.)

Place	Date	Hour	Summary of Events and Information	Remarks and references to Appendices
HOLLEBEKE SECTOR	20/8/17		A gas bombardment or to enemy trenches during night. Y.S.O.R. Major Lons Dunne visited Bn H.Q. Quiet on front line. OPTIC TRENCH bombarded for 5 hours without doing any damage. Enemy put some gas shells but not over by the enemy near WHITE CHATEAU	
	21/8/17		Our guns and 5 artillery very active all day. Very few very quiet all day, also Enemy enemy. S.O.S. was sent up by the 12th Bn Royal Scots Regt. Who went the S.O.S was sent up in reserve to BOIS CONFLUENT. Casualties during night in front line very slight - 5 men wounded	
BOIS CONFLUENT	22/8/17		Lt CHAIZE reported sick. 3 wounds received in action on 21/7/17. 2/Lt H.H.HOMEWOOD, 2/Lt H.MILLS + 2/Lt J.R.BRADLEY R. joined Etc. Battalion + were posted to A,B + C companies respectively. Troops resting - working parties at night.	
	23/8/17		Battalion was relieved by the 17th Manchesters Regt. and marched via RIDGE WOOD	
RIDGE WOOD	24/8/17		Company and General. Some tapping Lewis &c.	

Army Form C. 2118.

WAR DIARY
or
INTELLIGENCE SUMMARY.
(Erase heading not required.)

Instructions regarding War Diaries and Intelligence Summaries are contained in F. S. Regs., Part II. and the Staff Manual respectively. Title pages will be prepared in manuscript.

Place	Date	Hour	Summary of Events and Information	Remarks and references to Appendices
RIDGE WOOD	25/8/17		Under Company arrangements. Camp inspected by Divisional Commander	
	26/8/17		Enemy H.V. Gun fired six rounds into camp between 7 & 8 a.m. No casualties in Battⁿ	
	27/8/17		The Battalion relieved the 1/1ˢᵗ Cambridgeshire Regiment in the KLEIN ZILLEBEKE left sector.	
KLEIN ZILLEBEKE	28/8/17		Very quiet in line all day. Reserve Coys working on trenches & dugouts	
	29/8/17		Unusually quiet day. Our guns did a lot of counter battery work	
	30/8/17		In a Coy relief on left Coy front. One rocket pistol captured by left front Coy (C Coy) from a Hun patrol	
	31/8/17		The Battalion was relieved by the 12ᵗʰ Royal Sussex Regiment & became Brigade in support in the O.B.L. & O.G.L. near Transport Corner	

A.K. Robinson
Major
O.C. 13ᵗʰ R.Sus.R.
1ˢᵗ Sept 1917

Original

116/39
13 R. Sussex Regt
Vol 19

WAR DIARY
or
INTELLIGENCE SUMMARY.
(Erase heading not required.)

Army Form C. 2118.

Instructions regarding War Diaries and Intelligence Summaries are contained in F. S. Regs., Part II. and the Staff Manual respectively. Title pages will be prepared in manuscript.

Place	Date	Hour	Summary of Events and Information	Remarks and references to Appendices
KLEIN ZILLEBEKE	1/9/17		Resting during day. All Coys in working parties during night.	
	2/9/17		Battalion was relieved by the 10th Loyal North Lancs Regt. and took over RIDGE WOOD	
	3/9/17		Numerous E.A. Battles fronts in adjacent wood during the night.	
	4/9/17		Inter Company arrangements - paths & gun emplacements.	
	7/9/17		Training under Company arrangement.	
	8/9/17		Training under Company arrangement.	
INKEWSWICK FOREST	8/9/17		Relieved 1st 4th Black Watch on Tenasserim Front (right sub-sector)	
	9/9/17		Enemy Artillery active during period on observed enemy movement in break area. T.M's when fired on resumed firing at J25 d 33.97. The front revealed their objective such the enemy failed to resume. Behind support fronts were moved T.M's sights in only so that it could not be observed there at enemy battery. The enemy returned of the R.E.S derailed the Batty regist'd the loss of ammunition, after the 2nd Lt NOTT I.E. who went forward with the working party much under his cloth on reaching objective	D 19

WAR DIARY
or
INTELLIGENCE SUMMARY.

(Erase heading not required.)

Army Form C. 2118.

Instructions regarding War Diaries and Intelligence Summaries are contained in F. S. Regs., Part II. and the Staff Manual respectively. Title pages will be prepared in manuscript.

Place	Date	Hour	Summary of Events and Information	Remarks and references to Appendices
DIKKEBUSCH FOREST	9/9/17	9/9/17	It was beyond doubt largely due to their unfortunate event that the raid was not carried through to a complete success. Front line support lines cleaning all available dugouts & were to etc Reserve (comprising carrying rations water) Enemy artillery active on support & reserve lines dropping gas shells. Their were strong whizz bang & rd. rea shoots but these were of a two light with much enemy plane. Enemy plane at low feet up fuel M.S. a m forl line covering our whole front. Enemy artillery very active. Hs shrapnel very generally & gas shells (mineral towers) in persons compounds with cross openings. Our artillery work but fair & inferior	
	12/9/17		Bn relieved by 16th Bn Liverpool Regt & went back to RIDGEWOOD CAMP	
	13/9/17		Inspection parades and modents Baths	

Army Form C. 2118.

WAR DIARY
or
INTELLIGENCE SUMMARY.
(Erase heading not required.)

Instructions regarding War Diaries and Intelligence Summaries are contained in F. S. Regs., Part II. and the Staff Manual respectively. Title pages will be prepared in manuscript.

Place	Date	Hour	Summary of Events and Information	Remarks and references to Appendices
RIDGEWOOD	14/9/17		Training under Battalion arrangements	
	15/9/17		do. Relieved 16th Notts & Derby Regt in SHREWSBURY FOREST sector. Relief completed 11.20 p.m.	
SHREWSBURY FOREST	16/9/17		2nd Lt WRIGHT & 20 men raided enemy dug outs near LONE STAR POST.	
	17/9/17		Our artillery harassed the enemy 24 hrs, enemy reply feeble.	
	18/9/17		do	
	19/9/17		Battn relieved by 17th Notts Derby Regt & 16th Rifle Brigade. Relief complete by 6.15 a.m. Battn went by bus to BROKE CAMP	
N.9.b.	20/9/17		Battn moved up at 7 p.m. to trenches at N.9.b. in reserve	
	21/9/17		Time spent in improving camp and training	
	22/9/17		Relieved fragments of 41st Division in TOWER HAMLETS sector. Reorganised lines for assembly positions	
	23/9/17		Relieved by 11 R Sussex Regt and 12 R Sussex Regt and 8th (Res 1 company) relieved to RIDGEWOOD at 10.30 a.m. & reorganised	
	24/9/17		Battn moved up to assembly position in TOWER HAMLETS sector. Relief completed by 11 P.M. relieving the 12 Royal Sussex Regt.	

WAR DIARY
or
INTELLIGENCE SUMMARY.

(Erase heading not required.)

Army Form C. 2118.

Place	Date	Hour	Summary of Events and Information	Remarks and references to Appendices
TOWER HAMLETS	26/9/17		B⁰ attacked at 5.50 P.M. and captured all objectives 2nd + 4th Objs.	
	27/9/17		Proceeded with consolidation of position assisted by 3 Companies of 17th NOTTS & DERBY R⁰⁰. Relieved by 10th R.W.K.	
			FUSILIERS relief complete by 1 A.M.	
FRONTIER CAMP	28/9/17		B⁰ proceeded by Light Rly to FRONTIER CAMP near WEST HOUTHEM	
			Day spent in rest & cleaning up.	
	29/9/17		B⁰ bathed. Reorganization commenced	
	30/9/17		Brigade Church parade in 12 Corps Sports ground. Reorganization continued.	

H.T.K. Robinson Lt Col.
O.C. 13th Royal Sussex Regt.
2 Oct 1917.

Original

* 13th R¹ SUSSEX REGT

Army Form C. 2118.

Instructions regarding War Diaries and Intelligence
Summaries are contained in F. S. Regs., Part II.
and the Staff Manual respectively. Title pages
will be prepared in manuscript.

WAR DIARY
or
INTELLIGENCE SUMMARY.
(Erase heading not required.)

Vol. 20

Place	Date	Hour	Summary of Events and Information	Remarks and references to Appendices
FRONTIER CAMP	1-10-17		Training under company arrangements. Inspection of companies by C.O. followed by some work on improvement of camp. Trenches dug round tents. Indent under Company arrangements. Inspection on by Major General Cunny.	
	2-10-17		on 13th Royal Sussex parade grounds.	
	3-10-17		Training under company arrangements. Work on improvement of camp. Trenches dug round tents.	
	4-10-17		Companies fired at Range. 2/Lt V.C. de Belle reported to Battn. such Street 9th Trench	
	5-10-17		Training under company arrangements. Gas demonstration to Brit Group offrs. Inspection at Range. Baths.	
	6-10-17		Inspection of companies by C.O. Training under company arrangements	
	7-10-17		Owing to bad weather no church parade could be held	
	8-10-17		Training under company arrangements. Route Boulogne Route. Paris in afternoon. Baths.	
	9-10-17		Battalion Route march in morning. Training under company arrangements. 2/Lt. H.L. BOTHATLY joined for duty. Revolver Shooting. Battalion Route march in	
	10-10-17		Training under company arrangements. Revolver Shooting. Afternoon Firing at Range. 2/Lt. R.F. BROWN joined for duty.	D.20

Army Form C. 2118.

WAR DIARY
or
INTELLIGENCE SUMMARY.
(Erase heading not required.)

Instructions regarding War Diaries and Intelligence Summaries are contained in F. S. Regs., Part II. and the Staff Manual respectively. Title pages will be prepared in manuscript.

Place	Date	Hour	Summary of Events and Information	Remarks and references to Appendices
FRONTIER CAMP	11-10-17		Bath Route March. Training under company arrangement. Revolver shooting. 2/Lt H E BURDGE joins for duty. 7 other ranks joined for duty.	
	12-10-17		Battalion Route march. Specialist training. 1 man joined for duty.	
	13-10-17		Training under company arrangements.	
	14.10.17		Reconnoitring by B.O. 2ic. Company Commanders + platoon sergeants of line to be taken over in TOWER HAMLETS sector.	
TOWER HAMLETS	15.10.17		Battalion relieved 10th York + Lancs Regt. (in support)	
Huston.			Relief complete by 10 p.m.	
	16.10.17		Improvement of lines and shelters carried out. Enemy artillery very active.	
			Burial of dead carried out.	
	17.10.17		Burial of dead continued. Prisoner asked from SHREWSBURY FOREST. Enemy artillery very active on tracks &c.	
			Relieved 14th Hants in front line. Left front Battalion.	
	18.10.17		Left front Coy accounted for 6 of the enemy by L.G. rifle fire. Right front Coy claimed 12. German killed relief apparently being	

Army Form C. 2118.

WAR DIARY
or
INTELLIGENCE SUMMARY.
(Erase heading not required.)

Instructions regarding War Diaries and Intelligence
Summaries are contained in F. S. Regs., Part II.
and the Staff Manual respectively. Title pages
will be prepared in manuscript.

Place	Date	Hour	Summary of Events and Information	Remarks and references to Appendices
			Carried out	
	19-10-17		Enemy Snipers and machine guns very active from LEWIS HOUSE and isolated dugout opposite Right Battalion.	
			Posts linked up by trench. Possible to visit left front coy by day. Heavy enemy barrage on line of BASSEVILLEBEEK, assumed to have been caused by the presence of large party who were burying cable and ascertain before dark. 1 officer wounded. 1 O.R. Killed + 2 O.R. wounded.	
			Relieved by 16th Notts + Derby Regt. Relief complete 12-30 a.m. Henry enemy shelling during whole night. Went via walking wounded.	
BEGGAR'S REST CAMP	20.10.17		Morning spent in rest. Reorganisation commenced. Improvements carried out in Camp.	
	21.10.17		Church services held in Camp.	
	22.10.17		Commanding Officers inspection. Clothes, boots + equipment inspected and incidents submitted for deficiencies. Baths. Feet rubbing and inspection.	
			11 other ranks joined for duty.	
	23.10.17		Relieved by 8th Devons and marched to BROKE CAMP. (Divisional Reserve).	

Army Form C. 2118.

WAR DIARY
or
INTELLIGENCE SUMMARY.
(Erase heading not required.)

Instructions regarding War Diaries and Intelligence Summaries are contained in F. S. Regs., Part II. and the Staff Manual respectively. Title pages will be prepared in manuscript.

Place	Date	Hour	Summary of Events and Information	Remarks and references to Appendices
BROKE CAMP	24.10.17		Tents noah. notted. 1 O.R. joined for duty.	
	25.10.17		Improvements carried out. Training under Company arrangements.	
	26.10.17		Training in accordance with programme.	
			do	
	27.10.17		2nd Lieuts L.G. Whistler and G.E. Thornton joined for duty. Training in accordance with programme.	
	28.10.17		Battalion Church parade. Relieved by 2nd M.A.C. and marched to MURRUMBIDGEE CAMP (N.7.a.4.9.) taking over from 1/1st Cambridgeshire Regt.	
MURRUMBIDGEE CAMP	29.10.17		Training under Company arrangements. Improvements carried out.	
	29.10.17		2nd Lt. Hooper, Hardwicke and Clements joined for duty.	
	30.10.17		Training in accordance with programme. Replica and model of enemy dugouts to be captured commenced.	
	31.10.17		Battalion route march. Replica and model of dugouts completed.	

[Signed] Major,
Commdg. 13th Rl. Sussex Regt.

Original

13 R Sussex
Army form C. 2118
Vol 21

WAR DIARY
or
INTELLIGENCE SUMMARY.
(Erase heading not required.)

Instructions regarding War Diaries and Intelligence Summaries are contained in F. S. Regs., Part II. and the Staff Manual respectively. Title pages will be prepared in manuscript.

Place	Date	Hour	Summary of Events and Information	Remarks and references to Appendices
MURRUMBIDGEE CAMP	1-11-17		Special operation by "B" Coy. Other coys. shell hole adaption practice and training under coy. arrangements. Baths.	
	2.11.17		"B" coy practicing special operation. Other coys. under Company Commanders 5 other ranks joined for duty	Min Brown (?)
TOWER HAMLETS (Left front sub section)	3.11.17		Battalion relieved the 1/1st Cambs Regt in this subsection - moving by bus to SHRAPNEL CORNER. Thence by route march. Relief complete 11-30 p.m.	
	4.11.17		Improvements to line and dugouts. Burial of dead proceeded with. Communication trenches to front coys. commenced. Dugouts occupied by Bn. H.Q. and Aid Post improved. T.M. fire and snipers very active from GHELUVELT, LEWIS HOUSE and LONE TREE dugouts. (This latter is not always in our use). Patrols reported ground very swampy in front of LEWIS HOUSE, and between Left and Right battalions	
	5.11.17		Work proceeded with. Dump found at KANTINTJE CABT. all rations and water brought to this dump. Enemy shelling of our line and MENIN ROAD Support trenches badly damaged and	D 2

A6945 Wt. W11422/M160 350,000 12/16 D.D. & I. Forms/C/2118/14.

Army Form C. 2118.

WAR DIARY
or
INTELLIGENCE SUMMARY.
(Erase heading not required.)

Instructions regarding War Diaries and Intelligence Summaries are contained in F. S. Regs., Part II. and the Staff Manual respectively. Title pages will be prepared in manuscript.

Place	Date	Hour	Summary of Events and Information	Remarks and references to Appendices
			casualties caused. Large number of gas shells sent over.	
	6.11.17		Very heavy enemy barrage along whole front causing several casualties. 2nd Lt. Sayers and Sgt. Sudman wounded whilst getting communication with Bde. H.Q. by lamp. All wires between Bn. H.Q. and Coys were cut, and communication very difficult. The actions of the Officers and N.C.O. ranks in endeavouring to restore communications under intense fire was most praiseworthy. Relief complete 12-15 a.m. and proceeded to CANADA STREET tunnels.	
CANADA STREET	7.11.17		Battalion in Brigade support. Relieved by 17th Notts and Derby Regt. Patrol sent up to reconnoitre LEWIS HOUSE under Lieut. Bennett, M.C. going very difficult, and patrol reported ground very swampy and wire in trenches in front of the dugouts. M.G. fire was opened on the patrol and LEWIS HOUSE appears to be strongly held. Marched to SHRAPNEL CORNER and entrained to CHIPPAWA CAMP.	
CHIPPAWA CAMP.	8.11.17		Rest and cleaning arms and accoutrements. Marched to MURRUMBIDGEE	

Army Form C. 2118.

WAR DIARY
or
INTELLIGENCE SUMMARY.
(Erase heading not required.)

Instructions regarding War Diaries and Intelligence Summaries are contained in F. S. Regs., Part II. and the Staff Manual respectively. Title pages will be prepared in manuscript.

Place	Date	Hour	Summary of Events and Information	Remarks and references to Appendices
MIRRUMBIDGEE	9.11.17		CAMP, relieving 4/5th Bn Black Watch. Baths in afternoon.	
CAMP.			Morning devoted to cleaning up. Inspection of Battalion by Comdg Officer in afternoon. Promulgation of F.G.C.M. on Pte Parato. 21 other ranks evacuated sick, struck off strength.	
	10.11.17		9 " " joined for duty, taken on strength of battalion. Battalion parade for distribution of ribbons for decorations awarded, by the B.G.C. Sports in afternoon. Rest.	
	11.11.17		Church parades. Rest.	
	12.11.17		Training in accordance with programme. Specialist training. Rest during afternoon. Football. Musketry. 6 O.R. joined for duty.	
	13.11.17		"A" & "B" Coys. Inspection by Comdg Officer. Practice attacks. "C" & "D" Coys. Musketry. Football and games in afternoon. 2/Lt Mosrop and 3 O.R. joined for duty.	
	14.11.17		Training under Battalion arrangements. Practice attacks carried out.	

Army Form C. 2118.

WAR DIARY
or
INTELLIGENCE SUMMARY.
(Erase heading not required.)

Instructions regarding War Diaries and Intelligence Summaries are contained in F. S. Regs., Part II. and the Staff Manual respectively. Title pages will be prepared in manuscript.

Place	Date	Hour	Summary of Events and Information	Remarks and references to Appendices
MURRUMBIDGEE CAMP	14.11.17		Revolver practice for all Officers and Lewis gunners.	
	15.11.17		Practice attacks; also carried out wearing box respirators. Firing demonstrations. Battalion drill. Football and boxing during afternoon. Improvements to camp in progress.	
	16.11.17		Training under Company arrangements. Firing in box respirators. Musketry for poor shots.	
			1st O.R. evacuated sick struck off strength.	
SCOTTISH WOOD	17.11.17		Battalion marched to Scottish Wood Camp, being relieved by 37th Bourn.	
CAMP	18.11.17		Improvements to camp commenced. Church Parade.	
	19.11.17		Day spent in improving camp; huts sandbagged, canvas built one Brigade mess started.	
			9 O.Rs. evacuated sick, church off. strength. 1 O.R. joined for duty.	
BEDFORD	20.11.17		Relieved 11th Bn. R. Suss Rgt. proceeding by march route.	
HOUSE CAMP.			Improvements to camp commenced.	
	21.11.17		'B' Coy. road-making KNOLL ROAD. Remainder of Battalion carrying R.E. material from CANADA STREET to front line, and wire working.	

Army Form C. 2118.

WAR DIARY
or
INTELLIGENCE SUMMARY.
(Erase heading not required.)

Instructions regarding War Diaries and Intelligence Summaries are contained in F. S. Regs., Part II. and the Staff Manual respectively. Title pages will be prepared in manuscript.

Place	Date	Hour	Summary of Events and Information	Remarks and references to Appendices
BEDFORD HOUSE	22.11.17		Working party "B" Coy roadmaking at KNOLL ROAD. Remainder of Battalion carrying & improving front line	
CAMP P.			Camp improvements continued. Extension to cookhouse built.	
			Duckboard walk and rubble tracks completed	
	23.11.17		Working parties as on previous days. Improvements continued	
			4 O.Rs examined sick and struck off strength	
			1 Officer and 3 ORs joined for duty & taken on strength.	
	24.11.17		Working parties as before.	
	25.11.17		Battalion relieved by 30? Div. and marched to DICKEBUSH siding. Entrained to GODWAERSVELDE thence by march route to WINNEZEELE area.	
WINNIZEELE	26.11.17		Training and improvements to billets	
	27.11.17		Training under company arrangements. Boxing and football	
	28.11.17		do	do	

Army Form C. 2118.

WAR DIARY
or
INTELLIGENCE SUMMARY.
(Erase heading not required.)

Instructions regarding War Diaries and Intelligence Summaries are contained in F. S. Regs., Part II. and the Staff Manual respectively. Title pages will be prepared in manuscript.

Place	Date	Hour	Summary of Events and Information	Remarks and references to Appendices
WINNIZEELE	29.11.17		Battalion relieved by 9th K.R.R.	
YPRES	30.11.17		YPRES march to CONVENT near Poperinghe took over 9th K.R.R. Billets Working parties etc. improving huts etc. Working parties A Coy unloading Iron Loopholes at HELL FIRE CORNER. D Coy Road Repairs at POLIZE CROSS ROADS. B Coy do at BAVARIAN HOUSE. C Coy and every other available man improving billets, sanitary arrangements etc.	

A6945 Wt. W14424/M1160 350,000 12/16 D. D. & I. Forms/C/2118/14.

Original

13th June 16.

Army Form C. 2118.

WAR DIARY
or
INTELLIGENCE SUMMARY.
(Erase heading not required.)

Jun 22

D.22

Place	Date	Hour	Summary of Events and Information	Remarks and references to Appendices
WIEHTJE	1/9/17		Proceeded by Buse route for the CONVENT, YPRES to WIEHTJE and relieves 108th Battalion R.E.	
	2/9/17		Battalion resumed their ordinary duty of dug-out construction. 1 Coy. working on trenching & dug-out making & one platoon E.P.S. worked dumb in orders to carry out by the steam-sawmill. Nil	
	3/9/17		Work on various ordinary duties as Coys. – Coy. dug outs, latrines constructed. 2 N.S. own horses. Coys & own camp.	
	4/9/17		Contemplated content.	
	5/9/17		"	
	6/9/17		"	
	7/9/17		Nothing day. Work continued as before. Very much around & over day.	
	8/9/17		Coys on completion of days work. Proceeded by road to POPERINGHE STATION entraining at ouselrd V.R.S. – Casualties – Nil.	
	9/9/17		Battalion debussed at Gare Grise, to POPERINGHE STATION, entraining as GODWAERSVELDE, debussed and proceeded on to march to billets at STEENVOORDE AREA. Arrived at about 12 noon.	

Army Form C. 2118.

WAR DIARY
or
INTELLIGENCE SUMMARY.
(Erase heading not required.)

Instructions regarding War Diaries and Intelligence Summaries are contained in F. S. Regs., Part II. and the Staff Manual respectively. Title pages will be prepared in manuscript.

Place	Date	Hour	Summary of Events and Information	Remarks and references to Appendices
STEENVOORDE	9/10/17		Inspection - Battalion turned out - Blues (girls, girls) Flares & Sand-bags inspected for units.	
	10/10/17		Battalion inspected by C.O. - 3 & 4 & 5 & 3 & 4 Platoons returned. Gas-helmet inspected with rest.	
COULOMBY	11/10/17		Bath in barn for C Coy 16 SODENAESNEUDE Platoon. Platoons was B Coy. Received as NEUVE-EGLISE area and relieved 10 Battalion COULOMBY & arrived at about 9 p.m.	
	12/10/17		Lects inverted by C.O. - Games - no religious service.	
	13/10/17		Company field conference (No. 95 LUMBRES) firing - Instructional carried out.	
	14/10/17		Great interest to us at RENINGHEM, Bren Cooker turning on companies when in action.	
	15/10/17		Firing on short Range.	
	16/10/17		Firing on + Range.	
	17/10/17		do	
	18/10/17		Firing on short Range.	
	19/10/17		Batts inspected by Brigadier General Lewis.	
	20/10/17		Firing on Short Range & Flexible Ladder.	

Army Form C. 2118.

WAR DIARY
or
INTELLIGENCE SUMMARY.
(Erase heading not required.)

Instructions regarding War Diaries and Intelligence Summaries are contained in F. S. Regs., Part II. and the Staff Manual respectively. Title pages will be prepared in manuscript.

Place	Date	Hour	Summary of Events and Information	Remarks and references to Appendices
COLOMBY	21		Inspection of Batt. by Major Gwadelews, and presentation of medal ribbons for fallen. In during recent operations	
	22		Practice attack on COLOMBY Dummy trenches	
	23		Church Parade. Capt. F.P.G. Williams attached to Battn. in M/O during absence of Capt. Rose on leave	
	24			
	25		Church Parade. Communion Service at 6.	
	26		Training. Baths at PENINGHEM.	
	27		Training. Instruction by Coy. Officers	
	28		Firing on Short Range. Batt. Bomb. Tournament	
	29		Training	
	30		Move to SIEGE CAMP - Bomb. moved to WIZERNES & entrained. Detrained at ELVERDINGHE moved to SIEGE CAMP	
	31		Training	

[signature]

Army Form C. 2118.

13 R Sussex
Vol 23

WAR DIARY
or
INTELLIGENCE SUMMARY.
(Erase heading not required.)

Instructions regarding War Diaries and Intelligence Summaries are contained in F. S. Regs., Part II. and the Staff Manual respectively. Title pages will be prepared in manuscript.

Place	Date	Hour	Summary of Events and Information	Remarks and references to Appendices
SIEGE CAMP	1.1.18		Training under Coy commanders. Musketry practice on short range for all Coys.	
	2.1.18		Training continued. Boxing and football competitions. Specialist training in afternoon.	
	3.1.18		Company training continued with musketry practice.	
	4.1.18		Reconnaissance of new sector by Officers and other ranks. Range practice for Lewis gunners. Programme of training obtained. Inspection of clothing and boots.	
	5.1.18		8 ORs struck off strength. 4 ORs taken on strength. Training continued. Specialists in afternoon. Games in afternoon.	
	6.1.18		Divine service. Front line reconnoitred by disabled parties.	
HILLTOP FARM	7.1.18		Battalion paraded at 5 am and proceeded to work at CORPS LINE.	D 23
	8.1.18		Afterwards took over camp from 1/1 Herts Regt.	"
	9.1.18		Working party of 3 Coys on WINCHESTER SWITCH. 1 Coy carrying rations	"
	10.1.18		"	"
	11.1.18		"	"

Army Form C. 2118.

WAR DIARY
or
INTELLIGENCE SUMMARY.

(Erase heading not required.)

Instructions regarding War Diaries and Intelligence Summaries are contained in F. S. Regs., Part II. and the Staff Manual respectively. Title pages will be prepared in manuscript.

Place	Date	Hour	Summary of Events and Information	Remarks and references to Appendices
HILLTOP FARM.	12.1.18		3 Coys. working on WINCHESTER SWITCH. 1 Coy. carrying materials	
	13.1.18		" " "	
	14.1.18		" " "	
WESTROOSE BEEK	15.1.18		Relieved 1/6 Cheshires in Right sub sector. Gale and abnormal rain-storm. Great difficulty in reaching front line posts owing to the PADDEBEEK being flooded - men waist off their feet. Arrived drenched through. Posts over knee-deep in mud and water. Relief complete 4 am 16th.	
SECTOR	16.1.18		Relieved right front coy. by support coy. Posts still very wet and muddy - and many men evacuated.	
	17.1.18		Left front coy. relieved by Reserve Coy. Posts improved somewhat but ground very wet and muddy. New track made from support line to right front.	
	18.1.18		Relieved by 12th Rl. Sussex Regt. and marched to HILLTOP FARM. 11 pm.	
HILLTOP FARM	19.1.18		Day spent in rest - foot rubbing and cleaning up.	
CORPS LINE.	20.1.18		Relieved the 16th Rifle Brigade. Relief complete by 8 am.	

Army Form C. 2118.

WAR DIARY
or
INTELLIGENCE SUMMARY.
(Erase heading not required.)

Instructions regarding War Diaries and Intelligence Summaries are contained in F. S. Regs., Part II. and the Staff Manual respectively. Title pages will be prepared in manuscript.

Place	Date	Hour	Summary of Events and Information	Remarks and references to Appendices
CORPS LINE	21.1.18		Latrines built and shelters improved. Relieved by 17th Royal Scots and marched to WIELTJE when entrained at 8 pm for RAILHOER.	
SCHOOL CAMP	22.1.18		Day spent in cleaning clothing and equipment. Foot rubbing parades.	
	23.1.18		Re-organising. Inspections. Issue of new clothing and boots.	
	24.1.18		Company training and inspections by C.O.	
	25.1.18		Baths for whole battalion. Coy training. Football in afternoon.	
	26.1.18		9 – 10.30 am Company training. Battn paraded for route march and entrained at Proven at 10pm 7.30 pm 106 ORs were sick and about ½ of strength. 2 VBs joined Indiv. as 15 km in stage	
Sailly Louette	27.1.18		Battn entrained at Peronne halts & proceeded by route march to Sailly Louette arriving about midday. Parade under Company arrangements. Saluting and statures on Parade.	
	28.1.18		Company training A + D Coys route march. Foot rubbing parades. Both pm 2170 ORs	
	29.1.18		Battn paraded at 2.45 pm and proceeded by route march to Cotte entraining at 6 pm	
	30.1.18		Detrained at Proven at 10.45 pm approx(?) by route march to Nord Allaines arriving midnight.	
Nord Allaines	31.1.18		Foot rubbing inspections under Coy arrangements	

W R Robinson Lt Col
O C 13th R S Fus

Army Form C. 2118.

13 R Leac B
Vol 24

WAR DIARY
or
INTELLIGENCE SUMMARY.
(Erase heading not required.)

Instructions regarding War Diaries and Intelligence Summaries are contained in F. S. Regs., Part II. and the Staff Manual respectively. Title pages will be prepared in manuscript.

Place	Date	Hour	Summary of Events and Information	Remarks and references to Appendices
HAUT ALLAINES	1-2-18		Bath parade at 8 A.D. and proceeded by route march and light railway to Etricourt	
CHURCH CAMP HEUDICOURT	2-2-18		CHURCH CAMP HEUDICOURT, to become Reserve Battn centre sub-section 39th Divl. Front. Parades under company arrangements. Improvements carried on in camp	
	3-2-18		Working parties provided at night in improving trenches. Fort working parades for whole of Battn. Camp improvements carried on. Two companies provided night working parties in line.	Miss sent
	4-2-18		Cleaning camp. Battn relieved 12th R. Sussex Regt. in Right Front sub-section of 39th Divl Front. Two companies A + C in front line. "D" Coy Support Coy and "B" Coy in reserve company. Relief complete by 9.30 p.m. Patrols sent out by front line companies. 6 Officers joined Battn for duty.	
RIGHT FRONT SUB-SECTOR	5-2-18		Posts improved and trenches cleaned. Wiring parties strengthened wire at night. Patrols and listening posts sent out. Training continues. Latrine accommodation improved.	
	6-2-18		Working parties provided daily by reserve and support companies. Trenches cleaned. Patrols sent out. Training continues. Salvage continues.	
	7-2-18		Work in trenches carried on. Training continues. Patrols sent out.	
	8-2-18		Trenches revetted and improved. Wiring parties pushed. Patrols sent out.	D.24

A6945 Wt. W1422/M1160 350,000 12/16 D.D. & L. Forms/C./2118/14.

Army Form C. 2118.

WAR DIARY
or
INTELLIGENCE SUMMARY.
(Erase heading not required.)

Instructions regarding War Diaries and Intelligence Summaries are contained in F. S. Regs., Part II. and the Staff Manual respectively. Title pages will be prepared in manuscript.

Place	Date	Hour	Summary of Events and Information	Remarks and references to Appendices
RIGHT FRONT SUB-SECTOR	9.2.18		"A" & "C" companies relieved by two companies of 1/1 Herts Regt in front line. 1/3rd R. Sussex Regt becoming Support Battalion. Relief complete by 10 p.m.	
	10.2.18		Fortifying posies by companies under supervision of T.O. 11 Officers and 200 O.Rs transferred from 13th R. Sx R, 9 of whom proceed for duty in line.	
	11.2.18		Working parties continue. Trenches cleared and improved. Salvage continues.	
	12.2.19		do. do.	
	13.2.18		do. do. Major A.E. Andrews took over command of Battalion on Lt Col H.T.K. Corwin D.S.O proceeding on leave. 50 O.Rs joined Battalion from Base.	
	14.2.18		A & C companies relieved two companies of 1/1 Herts Regt in line. 13th R. Sx R. becoming Right Front Battalion in line. Relief complete 9 p.m. Working parties in trenches and posts. Received Support companies provisions. Working parties, 7 O.Rs joined Battalion from Base. 10 O.Rs struck off strength. Patrols sent out on front line companies. Salvage continues.	
	15.2.18		Improvements and work carries on. Reconnoitring patrols sent out.	
	16.2.18		do.	

Army Form C. 2118.

WAR DIARY
or
INTELLIGENCE SUMMARY.
(Erase heading not required.)

Instructions regarding War Diaries and Intelligence Summaries are contained in F. S. Regs., Part II. and the Staff Manual respectively. Title pages will be prepared in manuscript.

Place	Date	Hour	Summary of Events and Information	Remarks and references to Appendices
RIGHT FRONT SUB-SECTOR	17.2.18		Work continues. Salvage continues. Improvements to Trenches. Working parties continue.	
	18.2.18		Batn relieved 1/ Herts Regt in Divisional Reserve. B. C. & D. Companies at REVELON FARM. 'A' Coy. at HEUDICOURT. Relief complete 10 p.m.	
DIVISIONAL RESERVE	19.2.18		Cleaning equipment etc. Parades under Company arrangements.	
	20.2.18		Batn at HEUDICOURT. Working parties on YELLOW LINE. REVELON FARM improved. Raid done on "C" Coy. on German PW. Found to be unoccupied. No identification taken. 1 Officer 130 O.R.Wounded.	
	21.2.18		Batn at FINS. Working parties on YELLOW LINE. Full marching parade. Batn in camp.	
	22.2.18		Footwearing continues. Working parties provided for YELLOW LINE. 68 O.R. joins for duty. 22 O.R. evacuated. Batn relieves 1/ Herts Regt in Right sub-sector. 'B' & 'C' Companies in line. A' & 'D' in Support. Relief complete 9.45 p.m.	
RIGHT FRONT SUB-SECTOR	23.2.18		Trenches + posts improved. Salvage continues. Working parties provided for from line. Strong posts, and for cable burying. Patrols sent out.	
	24.2.18		Work continues. Cable burying proceeded with. Post making continues.	
	25.2.18		Work continues on Strong Posts and trenches. Cable burying parties provided. Patrols sent out.	
	26.2.18		Work and salvage continues. A' & 'D' Companies relieves B. & C. in front line. Patrols sent out.	

Army Form C. 2118.

WAR DIARY
or
INTELLIGENCE SUMMARY.
(Erase heading not required.)

Instructions regarding War Diaries and Intelligence Summaries are contained in F. S. Regs., Part II. and the Staff Manual respectively. Title pages will be prepared in manuscript.

Place	Date	Hour	Summary of Events and Information	Remarks and references to Appendices
RIGHT FRONT SUB-SECTOR	27.3.18		Work continued. Strong posts and trenches improved. Reconnaissance continues.	
	28.3.18		do. do. do.	

J.E. ?????
Major
O.C 13th R Sussex R.

116th Inf.Bde.
39th Div.

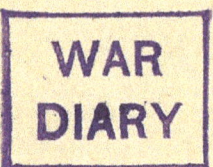

13th BATTN. THE ROYAL SUSSEX REGIMENT.

M A R C H

1 9 1 8

WAR DIARY
or
INTELLIGENCE SUMMARY.
(Erase heading not required.)

Army Form C. 2118.

13 R Sussex R
8/4/18

Place	Date	Hour	Summary of Events and Information	Remarks and references to Appendices
Right Sector Villers-Carbonel	1/3/18		Work continued. Battle patrols in yellow line occupied by 10 pm in front of parapet attack on Battle positions improved. Relieved by 11 Herts.	
	2/3/18		Moved to Reserve at Rosières Farm. Battle positions in yellow line occupied at night	
	3/3/18		" Working parties employed improving & wiring trench on yellow line	
	4/3/18		" Working parties A & B Coys provided to proceed Battalion Ration	
	5/3/18		Sent R. for S.O.S. at 5.15am Relieved 11 Pt Sussex N Front Section	
	6/3/18		A/B in front line. Work on positions continued	
	7/3/18		C/D relieved A/B in afternoon about 4.30. Quiet night	
	8/3/18		Raid by left battalion at 9pm. 2 stout fighting patrols sent out & found enemy trenches strongly held	
	9/3/18		Enemy bombardment changed to drum fire at 11 pm	
	10/3/18		Usual trench routine throughout.	
	11/3/18		" Notified Brigade would be relieved following day	
	12/3/18		Relieved at night by South Lancashire. 9th Division proceeded to yellow wood by tram	
	13/3/18		9 R.O. were in Yellow Wood. Cleaning up & refitting	
	14/3/18		Moved in afternoon to Grand Camp Villers Faucon. Work generally Brunehamel	
	15/3/18		Working parties as above	
	16/3/18		Moved to Hamel near Tincourt	
	17/3/18		Lt Col Johnson took over command. Reinforcement from Base. Working Parties	
	18 & 20		Working Parties	
	21/3/18		Heavy bombardment commenced in early hours. Ordered to endeavour at Jules Wood. Moved then	
2nd Battle of Somme	22/3/18	9am	Enemy attacked at 9am & were driven off, but took up positions on Bunker line adroit to form a defensive flank. About noon enemy made strong attacks on this H.Q. occupied jointly with 1st Herts. at quarry N 18 6 and this they were repulsed. Orders were shortly received to withdraw to Green line. This movement was successfully carried out & but A.G. with 1/2 B Coy who had been sent up with their own and ? ammunition, 4 officers & about 150 O.R. were thus lost to the Battalion. The night was fairly quiet	D 25

WAR DIARY or INTELLIGENCE SUMMARY

Army Form C. 2118.

Place	Date	Hour	Summary of Events and Information	Remarks and references to Appendices
2nd Battle of Somme (Contd)	23/3/18		Battn ordered to evacuate green lines & take up position about 3 miles E. of Pozieres, & cover withdrawal of 117.118 Bdes. Owing to inability of infantry to reach their previous get rounds further flanks, it was necessary to fall back in previous position T.N. in echelon. Retreat successfully accomplished though previous ridge held until blown up by Sappers during this day. The Bn again suffered heavy casualties.	
	24/25		Remnants of Bn incorporated in composite Bn by orders of G.O.C. the Army & fought with them throughout day.	
	24/3/18 25/3/18		Reformed 116 Bde & defended Chipilly during enemy advance of 117.118 Bde. Bn ordered to different thousand but enemy succeeded in crossing canal about 1½ miles in rear & Bn was ordered to try & cut them off, but arrived too late. A counter attack was launched & the Bn drove enemy back about 1000 yds, but no supports or ammunition arriving were compelled to fall back to position about 1 mile E. of Lamotte.	
	28/3/18		Bn ordered to withdraw and cover 1 Late of arrival of rations became heavily engaged, only with difficulty got past a position between Morlancourt & Mericourt, where of withdrawal position 500 yds E. of Morlancourt.	
	29/3/18		Remained in this position until evening when relieved by troops of 61st Division & moved to Heilly.	
	30/3/18		Took part in counter attack near Hamegard, & might ordered to withdraw & occupied at Heilly.	
	30/3/18 4/4/18 2/4/18 3/4/18 4/4/18		Moved in lorries to Querrieu & billets there. Arrangement staying. Moved to Mericourt-Abbeville by march route. Marched to Montjoie. Remained there refitting until marched to Heliocourt.	

W.T.F. R.S..........

39th Division.   116th Brigade.

Composite Brigade

Formed part of No. 2 Composite Battalion 10.4.18.

1/13th BATTALION

ROYAL SUSSEX REGIMENT

APRIL 1918.

WAR DIARY

of 13th Bn R Sussex Regt

for April 1918

Vol 26

Place	Date	Hour	Summary of Events and Information	Remarks and references to Appendices
GUIGNEMCOURT	1-4-18		Battalion Resting after 2nd Battle of Somme.	
	2-4-18		Move to Fericourt en Vimeu by Road Route.	
	3-4-18		Marched to MOUFLIERS remained there resting	
	4-4-18		Marched to HELLOUR.	
	5-4-18		Marched to EU and entrained for ARQUES.	
	9-4-18		Arrived ARQUES - & marched to TILQUES.	
	10-4-18		Ordered forward to VLAMERTINGHE and entrained at St OMER at 2 A.M. 11th arrived VLAMERTINGHE & T.A.M. & marched to OTTAWA Camp	Strength
			OTTAWA Camp. Battalion made up to Strength by 13 Officers and 270 fin 724 O.R.
			368 Men of 13th Bn Ybresister Regt (Pioneers) and one to 2Bn of the 39th Division Composite Brigade. The Battalion was Commanded by Lt Col H.T.R. Potowine D.S.O. 13th B Sussex Regt with transport and Battalion Headquarters at 13/13 R Sussex Regt
	11-4-18		OTTAWA Camp. attacked to 21st Division	
	12-4-18		Moves by light Railway to Guxen Camp near Raxen Segard and held in Divisional Reserve the Camp was visited by Cavalry during daylight from 9 - 4 - 2 - 30 pm. no Casualties. Shelter & Bourdon during daylight	D 25

WAR DIARY or INTELLIGENCE SUMMARY

Army Form C. 2118.

Place	Date	Hour	Summary of Events and Information	Remarks and references to Appendices
CHATEAU SEGARD	13/4/18		Reserve Camp: Misty morning. Battalion stand at 15 minutes notice to move. At 4 p.m. Battalion orders to be ready to Ridge Wood at once, in order that they may be available for the 9th Division, in case of enemy breaking through. WYTSCHAETE Ridge Wood. All quiet.	
	14/4/18 15/4/18		Ridge Wood. Stand to at 4 A.M. Shelling of wood commenced about 4-45 A.M. Continued up to about 7 P.M. Camp was evacuated the Bn being accommodated in Trenches. Casualties 2 Killed & about 13 15 wounded.	
	16/4/18		Trenches in Ridge Wood. At 2 A.M. received orders to proceed to ROSSIGNOL Camp, and came under orders of Br. 62nd Infantry Brigade, under which we moved up to 20/21. Opn. At 10 A.M. the Bn was ordered to assemble for a counter attack, orders were to take place at 11 A.M. at WYTSCHAETE this was cancelled at the last moment. Fresh orders for counter attack were issued for 4-30 P.M. in conjunction with a French Division on the RIGHT Flank.	

WAR DIARY or INTELLIGENCE SUMMARY

Army Form C. 2118.

Place	Date	Hour	Summary of Events and Information	Remarks and references to Appendices
WYTSCHAETE	16/6		The Seaforths Reinforced by No. 3 Company B[n] on the left. The Bat[n] was moved forward with the 2nd Guards to the line VANDAMME FARM — LAGACHE FARM — STORE FARM. It took part in the Counter attack on the evening of the 16th to re-occupy MEDELSTEDE F[m] and WYTSCHAETE WOOD. Advancing under heavy M-G fire, both supporting and frontal, and seeing the first objective, to press further on the night, it was therefore impossible to press further. The line was then consolidated under very adverse conditions before the attack to reconnaissance of the ground had taken place.	
WYTSCHAETE	17/6		Aug[t] 17/18. The Battalion took over the line from VANDAMME F[m] to STORE F[m] relieving the 2nd Scotch Reg[t] & Irish Fusiliers.	
	18/6		— do —	
	19/6		Situation remained the same.	

Army Form C. 2118.

WAR DIARY
or
INTELLIGENCE SUMMARY.
(Erase heading not required.)

Instructions regarding War Diaries and Intelligence Summaries are contained in F. S. Regs., Part II. and the Staff Manual respectively. Title pages will be prepared in manuscript.

Place	Date	Hour	Summary of Events and Information	Remarks and references to Appendices
WYTSCHAETE	20/15		On the night of 20/21st the Battn. was relieved and proceeded to Walker Camp. During the operations from 16th to 20th the Battn. were constantly subjected to heavy shell and machine gun fire. 4 Officers and 130 other Ranks were lost to the Battalion.	4/13 2nd Lt [?] 2/Lt Green Killed Burns 2/Lt [?] 2/Lt R.S. Daly Killed 17.6.17 2/Lt J. Simpson Wounded 6.6.17 13 Ch[?]
Walker Camp	21/15		At 9 A.M. Moved out of the Camp, and again arriving at Dominion Camp. Casualties 30 OR received orders to proceed about 5 P.M. the night was quiet — and the Battalion rested.	wounded
Dominion Camp	22nd to 24th		Resting. Proceeded by Light Railway to BELZENWALLE which is opposite ZILLEBEKE. Relieving the 16th Bn. Royal Irish Rifles in Reg.2 at Spoil Bank & Ritson Farm on the night 24/25.	
	25th		Watching the BLUFF on the E. side of Canal. At 2.30 P.M. the enemy opened a very heavy bombardment, employing H.V. guns with a considerable amount of gas shell. The enemy attacked about 4.15 P.M. the right from Company "B" covering the front of the attack. One platoon being	

Army Form C. 2118.

WAR DIARY
or
INTELLIGENCE SUMMARY.
(Erase heading not required.)

Place	Date	Hour	Summary of Events and Information	Remarks and references to Appendices
Spoil Bank	25/4		Annihilated, the other forces broke through TRIANGLE WOOD. The heavy mist, favoured the enemy in his attack. Enemy shelling continued throughout the day. Orders were received that 2 Companies of the 16th B'n would arrive in support, and be placed under the orders of Lt. Col. H.T.K. Robinson D.S.O. — These Companies did not report. Being in position until 3 A.M. 26th April. — Orders being received that the line BUS HOUSE — THE BLUFF — was to be held at all cost.	
do	26/4		Enemy Riflemen 13 B Glöwester Reg.2 was wounded. Hanging out the sign Bn 23/26. He B oneñion was heavily shelled out at 3 a.m. & 4 a.m. on the 26; retaliation was asked for. At 5 a.m. reports were received from the front line, showing enemy to be preparing for attack, a very heavy bombardment at the time at — 5.30 a.m. the S.O.S. was sent through by wire, as reply being received. The enemy meanwhile his apparently altered on the right, the line held by the Battalion not being engaged. —	

WAR DIARY or INTELLIGENCE SUMMARY

Army Form C. 2118.

Place	Date	Hour	Summary of Events and Information	Remarks and references to Appendices
Spoil Bank	26/9		At 7.30 A.M. Strong parties of the Enemy were seen approaching Bn Head Qrs at Spoil Bank. the mist enabling him to approach within 50 yards unseen, the alarm was given and the men ordered to take up position on the top of Spoil Bank. before the covered bn carried out the enemy had gained the Bank and surprised Bn Head Qrs to intense Rifle and Machine Gun fire. The mist prevented the Coy on the Bluff from seeing and rendering assistance. The result of the mist that only 3 Officers and about 10 OR of Bn Headquarters escaped — the remainder with the exception of 1 Officer & 20 men of C & 13 Bn Gloucester Regt 2 who gallantly held the Bluff — were either killed, wounded, or Captured — EO H T K Robinson being believed to be killed. The Command of 4/5 Bn being taken over by Capt G. I. Ritchie M.C. The Officer & men of the Gloucester Regt 2 who held the Bluff eventually managed to cut our way towards Hoplines — fighting their way back to our lines — Remaining Strength 1 Officer + 17. O.R.	

Army Form C. 2118.

WAR DIARY
or
INTELLIGENCE SUMMARY.
(Erase heading not required.)

Instructions regarding War Diaries and Intelligence Summaries are contained in F. S. Regs., Part II. and the Staff Manual respectively. Title pages will be prepared in manuscript.

Place	Date	Hour	Summary of Events and Information	Remarks and references to Appendices
Spoil Bank	24.6.16		The following casualties occurred in the 13th Bn Gloucester Regt	
			Lieut Homer & C. Killed	
			1 Major H R Howman missing	
			1 Capt. Burger Wheeler do	
			1 Capt. G.H. Hole do	
			1 2nd F.B. Whitaw do	
			do Hague do	
			do L. C. Farr do	
			1 Lieut A C Baker do	
			1/2 S Pawsey do	
			d S F Herring do	
			d S. Smith do	
			Temp' Lieut Wall was the only surviving Officer of the Battalion.	

WAR DIARY
or
INTELLIGENCE SUMMARY

Army Form C. 2118.

Place	Date	Hour	Summary of Events and Information	Remarks and references to Appendices
Sper Bank	26/9/16		The following Officers Casualties Occurred.	
			13th B'n R. Sussex Regt.	
			T/Lt Col H T Roy Robinson DSO Missing believes Killed	
			T/2 Lieut H C Harvey Missing	
			T Lieut L H Stott — do —	
			T/2 Lieut F J Lowdeu — do —	
			On the 27th inst. the 26th the following were the only surviving officers of the 13th B'n R Sussex Regt	
			T Capt & A/ Rothschild h C	
			Lieut R G Cooper	
			T do Q P Grace	
			T Lieut J D Thornthwaite Transpt Officer	
			Ma Low F N Rother Q M	
			Temp Lt. D J Valentine R A M C (attached)	

Army Form C. 2118.

WAR DIARY
or
INTELLIGENCE SUMMARY.
(Erase heading not required.)

Place	Date	Hour	Summary of Events and Information	Remarks and references to Appendices
At VOORMEZEELE	26/1/18		The remnants of 2 Corporals Batt. reported to the Officers Camp to the Batt. for Duty at 3-p.m. As the party only consisted of 7 Rifles they were stripped of their use as reinforcements and were ordered by O.C. to + Bt. to proceed to Transport lines at A.20. Camp which was received on arrival. One Officer + about 30 O.Rs. arrived at the Camp during the evening. Also 2 Officers of 13' B. Gloucester Regt. reported for duty from the newly reorganised Camp. The Strength of the Batt. then amounted to 6 Officers + 83 O.R.s including Transport. 8 Officers + 153 O.R's. During the day the Camp was Shelled at Intervals & the Transport was ordered to move —	
A.20 Camp	27/1/18			

Army Form C. 2118.

WAR DIARY
or
INTELLIGENCE SUMMARY.
(Erase heading not required.)

Place	Date	Hour	Summary of Events and Information	Remarks and references to Appendices
A.70 Camp	28/8/18		The Camp was Shelled at Intervals during the day. Casualties 2 O.R.'	
do.	29/8/18		The Batln. received orders to amalgate with 2.3.8. under the Command of Lt Col. R Wilkinson DSO Worcester Regt. 5 Officers + 83 O.Rs. proceeded to join 2.3.3.' at Dominion Camp.	
Dominion Camp	30/8/18		Orders were received for the Composite Brigade to be formed into 2 Battns. - the Elements of 2. 2 Battn. together will 3.8.' and the 11th Queens Regt. forming to 1 Br. under Lt Col. R Wilkinson DSO as Compos. Officer; with Capt. E.J. Rothschild M.C. as Second-in-Command.	

Sgd M.Hatchett Captain
Comdg 13th Bn Rhona Regt.

Army Form C. 2118.

WAR DIARY
or
INTELLIGENCE SUMMARY.
(Erase heading not required.)

Nov 27

Place	Date	Hour	Summary of Events and Information	Remarks and references to Appendices
Dominion Camp	1/5/18		The Battalion was serving with the Composite Battalion formed from the remainder of 6 Battalions under Lt Col Wilkinson with Capt Mitchell 2nd in Command. Orders were received to occupy a Green Line near Dickebusch.	
Green line Shdebusch	2/5/18		Brigade line all day, reconnoyance returned to Dominion Camp in evening.	
	3/5/18		Reoccupied Green line at 4 am. Returned to Dominion Camp at 10 p.m. & received orders to immediately re-occupy Green Line.	
	4/5/18		Marched to Camp in billets in Dominion Camp Annex to Linnelees Camp on Proven Road.	
	5/5/18	6/5/18		Marched to Rookruygge. Entrained at 6 p.m. for Audruicq. Arrived Audruicq. Composite Battalion dispersed into separate units. 13th Sussex billetted at Nielles. QM 3 Officers + 32 men returned from Ypres. These formed details and Wilk forming
Nielles lea Ardres	7/5/18		The operations not round Ypres. These formed details is Well forming a battalion of 11 Officers 202 O. Rs. Refitting.	

Army Form C. 2118.

WAR DIARY
or
INTELLIGENCE SUMMARY.
(Erase heading not required.)

Instructions regarding War Diaries and Intelligence Summaries are contained in F. S. Regs., Part II. and the Staff Manual respectively. Title pages will be prepared in manuscript.

Place	Date	Hour	Summary of Events and Information	Remarks and references to Appendices
Nellimbo Andres	9/5/18 to 23/5/18		Refitting & Training	
Nellimbo Andres	23/5/18		Formed into a Cadre Battalion, training staff remained. 7 officers B.S.O.R's proceeded to Etaples	
	24/5/18		Transport left for Base reinforcement of 1 Off. 44 ORs	
Bonningues	25/5/18		Marched to Bonningues Attached to Nos 1 & 3 Battalions of the 306 American Infantry Regiment	
" "	26/5/18 to 31/5/18		Instructional duties with the above	

G. M. Macdonell Major
O.C. 13th Stevens Res

WAR DIARY or INTELLIGENCE SUMMARY

Army Form C. 2118.

of 13th Bn Royal Sussex Regt

for June 1918

Place	Date	Hour	Summary of Events and Information	Remarks
Bonningues	1-6-18		Instructional duties with 1st & 3rd Bns. 57 & 306 American Infantry Regts.	
-"-	2-6-18		- do -	
-"-	3-6-18		- do -	
-"-	4 & 5th		- do - Lieut DOBBIE 6 'J' Infantry Same Regt.	
-"-	6-6-18		306th American Infantry Regt left Bonningues. Lieut Colonel C.H. Arman D.S.O. reported his arrival and took over command of the Battalion from Major E. Rotherwick D.S.O.	
-"-	7-6-18		Preparation for Move	
-"-	8-6-18		Battalion Staff moved to LICQUES.	
Licques	9 to 15th		Battalion Staff undergoing Training.	
-"-	16.6.18		Lt Col C.H.Arman D.S.O. took over the duties of Brigadier General of the 116th Infantry Brigade, during the absence on Leave of the Brigadier, Command of the Battn. devolved on Major E.Rotherwick. Battalion affiliated to 1st Battn. of the GRASSE FAYELLE and 120th American Infantry Regt for Instructional training.	
-"-	17.6.18			

Army Form C. 2118.

WAR DIARY
or
INTELLIGENCE SUMMARY.
(Erase heading not required.)

June (Cav.) 1918

Place	Date	Hour	Summary of Events and Information	Remarks and references to Appendices
Grasse Payelle	18.6.18		Instructional Duties with 1st Bath. Ahmed Infantry Regt.	
"	19.6.18 } 21.6.18 }	6	Moves with 1st Bn. A.I. Regt. to "B" Range for Musketry Course.	
"	22.6.18		Moves to Listergaur & attached to 2nd Bn A.I. Regt. (120th)	
Listergaur	23.6.18		2nd Lt P.E.N. Rothery reports for duty from hospital	
"	23rd & 25th		Moves with 2nd Bn 120th A.I. Regt to "B" Range for Musketry Course.	
"	26th		Instructional Duties at Listergaur.	
"	27th		— do — Lt. Col. C.H. Arrow D.S.O returned from Brigade	
"	28th		Heavy & Renewed Command of the B attacks	
"	29th		— do — Capt White M.C. to England on leave	
"	"		— do — 16 Recs F.R.P. Cannier C.F. joining for duty taken over from 11th Bn B.R. Servais	
"	"		attached to 1st Bn 120 Regt & 3rd Heugro. Duties taken over from 11th Bn B.R. Servais Regt. on their proceeding to England.	
"	30th		Instructional Duties with 1st & 2nd Bns. — No Recs reported for duty from "J" Base Depot. 2/Lt J.D. Dane reported for duty from 1st & 2nd Battns.	
"	"		Instructional Duties with 1st & 2nd Battns.	

Commanding 13th Bn. R. Sussex Regt. Lieut Colonel

Army Form C. 2118.

WAR DIARY
or
INTELLIGENCE SUMMARY.

(Erase heading not required.)

Of 13th Bn Royal Sussex Regt
1st July 1918
Vol 29

Instructions regarding War Diaries and Intelligence Summaries are contained in F. S. Regs., Part II. and the Staff Manual respectively. Title pages will be prepared in manuscript.

Place	Date	Hour	Summary of Events and Information	Remarks and references to Appendices
LISTERGAUX	1-7-18		Battalion Headquarters move to GRASSE PAYELLE. Other Ranks remain in Billets at LISTERGAUX.	
Grasse Payelle	2-7-18		Professional Authors of 1st & 2nd Bns 120th Regt. A.L. Regt. 120th Regt moves with 30th American Division to WATTEN. Col (H.Harman) D.S.O. accompanied Regimental Headquarters. Major C. Rothschild R.C., Capt Bradley R.C., Capt Jones, & Revd Jones acc. accompanied the 1st & 2nd & 2nd Bns of the 120- Regt. The remainder of the Battalion carried on training.	
"	3-7-18		Training of Instructors Continued	
"	4-7-18		- do -	
"	5-7-18		Lts Pr.F.X.D.Thos & Urwin engaged in Lect, by Capt Loring. Lt Col C.A. Harman D.S.O, Major S. Rothschild R.C., Capt. Bradley R.C., Capt Rue, & Lieut Jones R.C. Returned from 30th A.D. Division.	
"	6-7-18		15 Other Ranks from demonstration Platoon Joined for duty. Other Ranks of Battalion moved from LISTERGAUX to GRASSE PAYELLE. Lt Col Harman D.S.O. & Col Bradley R.C. proceeded to join 30th A.D. Division. for attachment as Instructors.	D

WAR DIARY
or
INTELLIGENCE SUMMARY.
(Erase heading not required.)

Army Form C. 2118.

July Courier 1918

Place	Date	Hour	Summary of Events and Information	Remarks and references to Appendices
Grasse Fayelle	7/7/18		2/Lt J.R. Jones + 6 Other Ranks to VII Corps School. Bombing + Musketry.	
"	8/7/18	11am	Daily programme of Training of Instructors Carried out:	
"	12/7/18		Lt Hutchinson & 4 Other Ranks MGO. to 1st Div Canon Pistol School at Leulinghem, as Instructors. Training of Instructors Continues.	
"	13/7/18		- do -	
"	14/7/18		Church Parade at Mielles Les Aaces.	
"	15/7/18		Capt Willie M.C. returned from leave. Training of Instructors Continues.	
"	16/7/18		Division Jackies Scheme.	
"	17/7/18		Lt Col Harvie DSO. Capt Bradley & 6 Officers from 2nd A.I. Division. Col C.H. Bolton M.C. returned from 116th Inf Bde Hdqrs.	
"			Capt Rode 2nd 39th Division Hqrs for duty. Training of Division Brigades	
"	18/7/18		- do -	
"	19/7/18		- do - Six Officers + 36 Other Ranks M.G. Corps attached	
"	20/7/18		- do - 2/Lt Jones + 6 Ors Rejoined from VII Corps School	
"	21/7/18		Church Parade at Mielles Les Aaces.	

WAR DIARY
or
INTELLIGENCE SUMMARY.
(Erase heading not required.)

Army Form C. 2118.

July Continued 191[?]

Place	Date	Hour	Summary of Events and Information	Remarks and references to Appendices
GRNSIS Paupelle	22/7		Training of Divisions Continued	
"	23/7		— do — Capt R.C. Cooper R.C. to 2nd Army Gas School, for Course	
"	23/7		— do — Battalion Tactical Exercise	
"	24/7		— do — Capt Rose rejoined from Division	
"			26 Issues proceeded to Base Depot, Struck off Battalion Strength	
"			Major G. Rothschild R.C. proceeded on Leave to Paris.	
"	25/7		6 Officers & 26 O.R. M.G. Corps proceeded to Base Depot	
"			Battalion moved to LIGQUES.	
LIGQUES	26/7, 27/7		Training of Divisions Continued. Tactical Exercises.	
"	28/7		Church Parade	
"	29/7		Training of Divisions Continued. 2nd Lt F.H. Robinson returned from Leave.	
"	30/7		— do —	
"	31/7		— do —	
"			Capt C.H. Bolton R.C. & 116 Infty Blue Herigo as Acting Staff Captain	
"			Capt R.C. Cooper R.C. Rejoined from 2nd Army Gas School	

Lt. Colonel
Commanding 13th Bn D[?] [illegible] Regt

WAR DIARY or INTELLIGENCE SUMMARY

Army Form C. 2118.

of 13th Bn. Royal Sussex
up to 14th August 1918.

Place	Date	Hour	Summary of Events and Information	Remarks and references to Appendices
Licques	1/8/18		Training	
"	2/8/18		-do- Lewis Gun Practice on Range.	
"	3/8/18		-do-	
"	4/8/18		Church Parade	
"	5/8 to 8/8/18		Training	
"	9/8/18		-do- Captains Rose & Bradley proceeded to England on leave.	
"	10/8/18		Capt. Rev. F.R. Barroff C.F. proceeded to join 32nd Divn.	
"	12/8 to 13/8/18		Rifle Competition at Battalion Range.	
"	14/8/18		Battalion transferred to 11th Bn. Royal Sussex Regt. marched to Audricq and entrained.	

L.E. Envis-Roper
Lieut Col
Comdg. 13th Bn. Royal Sussex Regt.

www.ingramcontent.com/pod-product-compliance
Lightning Source LLC
Chambersburg PA
CBHW081352160426
43192CB00013B/2393